University
of Michigan
Business
School Management Series

INNOVATIVE SOLUTIONS TO THE
PRESSING PROBLEMS OF BUSINESS

The mission of the University of Michigan Business School Management Series is to provide accessible, practical, and cutting-edge solutions to the most critical challenges facing business-people today. The UMBS Management Series provides concepts and tools for people who seek to make a significant difference in their organizations. Drawing on the research and experience of faculty at the University of Michigan Business School, the books are written to stretch thinking while providing practical, focused, and innovative solutions to the pressing problems of business.

Also available in the UMBS series:

Becoming a Better Value Creator, by Anjan V. Thakor

Achieving Success Through Social Capital, by Wayne Baker

Improving Customer Satisfaction, Loyalty, and Profit,
by Michael D. Johnson and Anders Gustafsson

The Compensation Solution, by John E. Tropman

Strategic Interviewing, by Richaurd Camp, Mary Vielhaber,
and Jack L. Simonetti

Creating the Multicultural Organization, by Taylor Cox

Getting Results, by Clinton O. Longenecker and
Jack L. Simonetti

A Company of Leaders, by Gretchen M. Spreitzer and
Robert E. Quinn

Managing the Unexpected, by Karl Weick and Kathleen Sutcliffe

Using the Law for Competitive Advantage, by George J. Siedel

Creativity at Work, by Jeff DeGraff and Katherine A. Lawrence

Making I/T Work, by Dennis G. Severance and Jacque Passino

Decision Management, by J. Frank Yates

A Manager's Guide to Employment Law, by Dana M. Muir

The Ethical Challenge, edited by Noel M. Tichy and
Andrew R. McGill

Competing in a Service Economy, by Anders Gustafsson and
Michael D. Johnson

For additional information on any of these titles or future
titles in the series, visit www.umbsbooks.com.

Executive Summary

Energy—the sense of being eager to act and capable of action—is a critical, limited, but renewable resource that enables excellence in individuals and organizations. Without effective means for generating and replenishing the energy of individuals in the workplace, no organization can ever be truly great.

Managers and leaders can make a profound difference in activating and renewing energy by building and sustaining high-quality connections with coworkers, bosses, subordinates, customers—anyone with whom they have contact at work. High-quality connections are marked by mutual positive regard, trust, and active engagement. They are connections in which people literally feel more alive and vibrant. They can be created in an instant—in a conversation, an e-mail exchange, or a meeting—and their effects can be powerful and long-lasting. High-quality connections contribute substantially to individuals' well-being and work performance. They also contribute significantly to an organization's capacity for collaboration, coordination, learning, and adaptation, as well as its ability to keep people committed and loyal.

Managers and leaders shape possibilities for energy in connection through two important means: how they interact with others and how they design and construct the contexts in which others interact. This book guides managers through both possibilities and offers concrete action suggestions for building these vitalizing connections.

Chapter One introduces the idea of connection quality and documents the far-reaching consequences of high- and low-quality connections for both individuals and organizations. The next three chapters each describe a pathway to building high-quality connections. Chapter Two focuses on respectful engagement and identifies a range of strategies for interacting in ways that convey messages of value and worth. Chapter Three focuses on task enabling as a potent set of strategies for taking actions that help another person to succeed and perform effectively. Chapter Four focuses on trust and details how managers build trust both by what they say and do and by what they refrain from saying and doing.

Management of connection quality also involves dealing constructively with low-quality connections that corrode individuals' sense of worth, competence, and value. These corrosive connections are all too prevalent in work organizations, and they leave major damage in their wake both for individuals and for the organization as a whole. Chapter Five identifies a range of strategies for reducing the damage of corrosive connections, and in some cases, transforming them into energy-producing as opposed to energy-depleting connections.

Chapter Six tackles the creation and design of contexts in which high-quality connections flourish. It examines key features of organizational context that influence the quality of connections, from organizational values to the design of physical space. The examination of these features reveals strategies managers and leaders can deploy to improve the climate for high-quality connections in their work group, department, unit, or organization.

Although this book is based squarely on research, it is written to be a practical guide. Each chapter provides abundant examples, detailed descriptions of actions to take, and assessments and other tools to help readers evaluate the quality of the connections in their workplace and take immediate steps to vitalize their work environment through the transformative power of high-quality connections.

Energize Your Workplace

How to Create and Sustain High-Quality Connections at Work

Jane E. Dutton

JOSSEY-BASS
A Wiley Imprint
www.josseybass.com

Published by Jossey-Bass
A Wiley Imprint
989 Market Street, San Francisco, CA 94103-1741   www.josseybass.com

Jossey-Bass books and products are available through most bookstores. To contact
Jossey-Bass directly call our Customer Care Department within the U.S. at 800-956-
7739, outside the U.S. at 317-572-3986 or fax 317-572-4002.

Jossey-Bass also publishes its books in a variety of electronic formats. Some content
that appears in print may not be available in electronic books.

Library of Congress Cataloging-in-Publication Data

Dutton, Jane E.
   Energize your workplace: how to create and sustain high-quality
connections at work/Jane E. Dutton.—1st ed.
        p. cm.—(University of Michigan Business School management
series)
   Includes bibliographical references and index.
      ISBN 0-7879-5622-8 (alk. paper)
   1. Reengineering (Management). 2. Communication in organizations.
3. Organizational change. 4. Management. I. Title. II. Series.
   HD58.87.D885   2003
   658.4'063—dc21

                                                    2003010517

Printed in the United States of America
FIRST EDITION
HB Printing   10 9 8 7 6 5 4 3 2 1

Contents

To my parents, Kate and George Dutton

Series Foreword

Welcome to the University of Michigan Business School Management Series. The books in this series address the most urgent problems facing business today. The series is part of a larger initiative at the University of Michigan Business School (UMBS) that ties together a range of efforts to create and share knowledge through conferences, survey research, interactive and distance training, print publications, and news media.

It is just this type of broad-based initiative that sparked my love affair with UMBS in 1984. From the day I arrived I was enamored with the quality of the research, the quality of the MBA program, and the quality of the Executive Education Center. Here was a business school committed to new lines of research, new ways of teaching, and the practical application of ideas. It was a place where innovative thinking could result in tangible outcomes.

The UMBS Management Series is one very important outcome, and it has an interesting history. It turns out that every year five thousand participants in our executive program fill out a marketing survey in which they write statements indicating the most important problems they face. One day Lucy Chin, one of our administrators, handed me a document containing all these statements. A content analysis of the data resulted in a list of forty-five pressing problems. The topics ranged from growing a company to managing personal stress. The list covered a wide territory, and I started to see its potential. People in organizations tend to be driven by a very traditional set of problems, but the solutions evolve. I went to my friends at Jossey-Bass to discuss a publishing project. The discussion eventually grew into the University of Michigan Business School Management Series— Innovative Solutions to the Pressing Problems of Business.

The books are independent of each other, but collectively they create a comprehensive set of management tools that cut across all the functional areas of business—from strategy to human resources to finance, accounting, and operations. They draw on the interdisciplinary research of the Michigan faculty. Yet each book is written so a serious manager can read it quickly and act immediately. I think you will find that they are books that will make a significant difference to you and your organization.

Robert E. Quinn, Consulting Editor
M.E. Tracy Distinguished Professor
University of Michigan Business School

Preface

My colleague Bob Quinn often knows things before I do. He had a strong inkling before I even dreamed of writing a book that I had something to say about energy and organizations. He challenged me to take what I know about building high-quality connections in organizations and use it to crack open a fundamental problem that all businesses face: how can leaders and managers produce energy and vitality as critical and renewable resources that make organizations and the people within them great?

This book is the result of this challenge. Abundant research suggests that a fundamental key to increasing energy in the workplace, and thereby increasing the effectiveness of both individuals and organizations, is the building of high-quality connections—ties between people marked by mutual regard, trust, and active engagement. A focus on high-quality connections and their energy-generating capabilities shows how small actions—such as respectful engagement with another person—can transform the energy possibilities in both people. It also highlights the role of managers like you in serving as role models and in designing contexts that enable these kinds of energy-generating connections to flourish.

The book stands on a solid foundation of research, but it is intended to be practical and useful, applicable to the everyday choices you make about how you interact with others. It offers tools for taking stock of your current connecting practices, and it invites you to consider alternative strategies that will better energize your workplace. It also asks you to consider how key features of the organizational context work to enhance or diminish the likelihood of high-quality connections. A wealth of examples illustrate the profound differences you can make in generating connections that build vitality and energy for yourself and for those you interact with at work—whether those persons are bosses, subordinates, customers, suppliers, or coworkers.

■ The Goals of This Book

When I say I am writing a book on energizing your workplace, people resonate. Very often they have a gut level reaction that registers, yes, I have experiences at work all the time that affect my energy and the energy of those around me. However, most of the stories they tell me are of connections that sap and deplete energy. I call these kinds of connections *corrosive.* They are all too prevalent in the workplace. Stories of organizations that drain and deaden are far more frequent than stories about organizations that revitalize and enliven. This reality has inspired me to set four goals for this book.

First, I want managers to seriously consider energy as a critical, limited, but renewable resource that enables excellence in individuals and organizations. Without effective means for generating and replenishing the energy of individuals in the workplace, no organization can ever be truly great. Further, no organization can retain the people it really wants to retain and have them achieve the levels of excellence they desire.

Second, I want managers to take their role as energy creators or energy depleters seriously. I also want them to see new possibilities for enlivening their workplace through building and enabling high-quality connections. This means having a perspective on how their everyday behaviors and their actions in designing the organizational context can create and replenish energy, contributing to all kinds of important outcomes, including employees' physical and psychological health, task engagement, learning, cooperation, coordination, attachment, and overall effectiveness.

Third, I want managers to have better and more abundant strategies for dealing with corrosive connections at work. Although low-quality connections infect most organizations, it's rare for anyone to have training or practice in how to deal with them constructively or coach others to do so.

Fourth, I hope this book convinces managers of the important connection between the quality of the connections they have at work and their overall well-being. The fact is that most of us spend a good percentage of our waking hours at our workplaces. In those places, we either are enlivened or deadened through the quality of the connections that we have with others. In the short run, these effects show up in performance and other organizationally relevant outcomes. In the long run, they leave lasting traces on our bodies and health. My greatest hope is that the managers who read this book will practice new ways of infusing vitality into the workplace by not only reducing corrosive connections but also increasing the frequency and vibrancy of high-quality connections. Their own lives depend on it.

■ Acknowledgments

I thank Bob Quinn for his initial challenge and the opportunity to meet the challenge through the writing of this book. Bob sees possibilities that other people do not dare to imagine, and he makes them happen. The UMBS Management Series is the end product of his vision in partnership with the Jossey-Bass team. I have benefited greatly from their creative vision and from the enabling and fine editing from John Bergez. I thank them all for their wonderful support in making this book happen.

No book is ever done alone. This book, in particular, was conceived jointly with Robert Holmes at the University of Michigan, who lives the content of this book on a daily basis. I benefited greatly from his mentorship and partnership in the initial structuring and writing. I hope he is pleased with the final product. Other University of Michigan staff members have also been instrumental in supporting the creation of this book. I would like to thank Maureen Burns, Mary Ceccanese, Dianne Haft, Sally Johnson, Paula Kopka, and Cynthia Shaw for their inspiration and instrumental help.

Many colleagues and both former and current students were invaluable in the book's creation. Jean Bartunek, Joyce Fletcher, Peter Frost, Christine Pearson, and Steve Stumpf read various drafts and offered wonderful insights and suggestions. Peter Frost provided significant encouragement through the entire journey of writing this book. Susan Bernstein and Laura Atlantis are two former MBA students who left lasting positive imprints on the book's content and structure. Steve Mondry, a former undergraduate student also provided useful feedback and examples. My faculty colleagues at the University of Michigan—Sue Ashford, Wayne Baker, Kim Cameron, Paula Caproni, Michael Cohen, Martha Feldman, Jane Hassinger, Maggie Lampert, Kim Leary, Bob Quinn, Gretchen Spreitzer, Kathie Sutcliffe, Jim Walsh, Karl Weick, Janet Weiss, Mayer Zald—are treasures who continuously enrich my work. My more distant colleagues—David Cooperrider, Kenneth Gergen, Connie Gersick, Jody Hoffer Gittell, Mary Ann Glynn, Karen Golden-Biddle, Hermi Ibarra, Rosabeth Moss Kanter, Sharon Lobel, Sally Maitlis, Joshua Margolis, Joanne Martin, Debra

Meyerson, Leslie Perlow, Anat Rafaeli, Huggy Rao, Brian Uzzi, Joe White—were also important inspirations. Former and current doctoral students contributed immensely to this book. The research done with Gelaye Debebe and Amy Wrzesniewski inspired the book's core thesis. For insightful discussions about high quality connections that gave me confidence to write from this perspective, I thank Caroline Bartel, Emily Heaphy, Jason Kanov, Katherine Lawrence, Jacoba Lilius, Regina O'Neill, Sandy Piderit, Ryan Quinn, Seung-Yoon Rhee, Laura Morgan Roberts, Nancy Rothbard, Markus Vodosek, Tim Vogus, Michele Williams, Monica Worline, and Joana Young. Cheryl Baker, Claudia Cohen, Anne Dutton Keesor, Alisa Miller, and Amy Saunders are friends and family who generously helped along the way. The MBA students in my "Managing Professional Relationships" class brought these ideas to life.

I also want to express my appreciation to the William Russell Kelly Chair, which has provided important financial support for me and my work, and to the University of Michigan Business School, which has proved to be a great learning, teaching, and researching environment.

To my husband, Lloyd (Lance) Sandelands, and to my daughters, Cara and Emily Sandelands: you three help me to know fully the meaning and significance of high-quality connections. Thank you for your unwavering support and inspiration during the writing of this book.

May 2003   Jane E. Dutton
Ann Arbor, Michigan

Energize Your Workplace

Creating Energy Through High-Quality Connections

This is a book about how leaders and managers in their everyday behaviors can make an enormous difference in activating and renewing the energy that people bring to their work. It is also about how to design and construct organizational contexts that produce energy and vitality as critical and renewable resources that make organizations (and the people within them) great.

The premise of this book is deceptively simple: the energy and vitality of individuals and organizations alike depends on the quality of the connections among people in the organization, and between organizational members and people outside the firm with whom they do business. The key to transforming both your own work experience and the performance of the people around you is to build and nurture what I call *high-quality* connections. This type of connection is marked by mutual positive regard, trust, and active engagement on both sides. In a high-quality connection, people feel more engaged, more open, more competent. They feel more alive.[1] High-quality connections can have a profound impact on both individuals and entire organizations.

One of the key insights that inspired this book is that a high-quality connection doesn't necessarily mean a deep or intimate relationship. High-quality connections do not require personal knowledge or extensive interaction. Any point of contact with another person can potentially be a high-quality connection. One conversation, one e-mail exchange, one moment of connecting in a meeting can infuse both participants with a greater sense of vitality, giving them a bounce in their steps and a greater capacity to act.

By the same token, low-quality connections exact a fearful toll on energy and well-being. Low-quality connections are marked by distrust and disregard of the other's worth. Such connections can dissolve our sense of our own humanity, competence, and worth, and they can do so in an instant. Like metal corroded through exposure to toxic substances, people in organizations are corroded through exposure to the toxicity of low-quality connections.[2] When low-quality connections are pervasive in an organization, they eat away at people's ability to learn, to show initiative, and to take risks. They corrode motivation, loyalty, and commitment.

In short, the quality of connections with others is one of the most powerful variables that influences the well-being of individuals and organizations alike. Before exploring this idea more formally, let me share two brief stories. They should give you a concrete feeling for the difference between high- and low-quality connections, and the enormous difference they make.

■ The Power of Connections: Two Brief Tales

Brian Sills was in charge of strategic planning at Phoenix Software. For some time he had been struggling to put a planning system in place that fit the fast-paced, lean, nonbureaucratic culture while still keeping people in all units headed in the same direction, aware of their long- and short-term strategic objectives. The task was demanding, but Brian accepted the challenge with zest. He bounced back from the occasional setbacks, energetically trying a new path.

Then Brian's boss, the vice president of Finance, left the company. The new VP proved to be a very uncommunicative manager. He responded to specific requests for information, but he did not include Brian in high-level meetings. He rarely consulted with Brian even when he was wrestling with strategic matters. From Brian's point of view, he seemed uninterested.

Initially, Brian gave little thought to his relationship with his new boss. The relationship wasn't effective, but at least it was not damaging. The connection became really corrosive when the VP reneged on promises and failed to provide assistance when Brian requested budgetary advice. He seemed to pay attention to Brian only when he had some criticism to impart. Brian spent an inordinate amount of time trying to figure out what he had done wrong. He actively sought advice from his peers about what to do. As his stress built, he found himself wrestling with frequent headaches and numbness in his left hand. His performance deteriorated as he began to feel less sure of himself and increasingly unwilling to share information with his boss. Instead of showing initiative, he kept his head down and focused on getting through the day.

As other staff members saw what was happening to Brian, the corrosion spread. Brian's colleagues started being more cautious about what they shared with the VP. Communication and trust plummeted in the unit. The VP knew that Brian's unit was developing "performance issues," but as far as he was concerned, the problem was with the staff. He had no idea of the effects his own malignant behavior was having on the people around him.

Does this scenario sound familiar? With a little thought, most of us can point to experiences like Brian's in our own work lives. Like Brian, we may have blamed ourselves when our performance and sense of well-being deteriorated. We may not have seen the real source of the problem—a corrosive connection.

Now consider the case of Gayle, a successful consultant in a well-known knowledge management consulting firm in Minneapolis. From the outside, Gayle's work life looked ideal. She made a great salary, traveled to exotic places, and was gaining more and more responsibility and recognition. She was well known as one of the high flyers at ABLE Consulting and was actively recruited by other consulting firms.

From the inside, Gayle's situation looked very different. She didn't think she was working excessively hard, yet most of the time she felt physically exhausted. When she wasn't working, she would find herself without energy to try the hobbies that she had been telling herself she would try when she found the right city, the right job, the right time. Interactions with others at work felt like mini-intrusions that were taking her away from the "real work" of her job. She found herself continuously apologizing for times she had been short with customers, unhelpful to colleagues who sought her out for help and advice, or unavailable to subordinates whom she saw as demanding and needy. She was starting to dislike her job and herself without any readily apparent reason.

Things turned around for Gayle when she received some very direct feedback from a long-term client. The client knew Gayle well enough to see that her unhappiness was growing, with costs to both Gayle and her unit as a whole. The client's advice was simple. He advised Gayle to take a different stand in the way that she thought about interacting with others. He suggested treating interactions as opportunities to build nourishing and replenishing connections—even if they lasted less than five minutes. He told Gayle that this form of interacting did not take a lot of work, but it did require a major change in attitude. It meant seeing and acting on the possibility that in every connection there was a wellspring of vitality to tap. It meant seeing the building of positive connections not as a waste of time but as the best investment she could make in her own well-being and sustained performance and that of her unit.

At first Gayle thought the advice was silly and overly simplistic, but she decided to give it a try. On her client's advice, she started small. The next day, on her way out of her apartment building, she happened to meet her mail carrier. Instead of brushing past him as she would normally do, she stopped and asked him how he was doing. It was the first time she had so much as made eye contact with him. With a smile, the mail carrier said he was doing just fine. He shared a brief story about his daughter's progress in school and said he hoped she'd grow up to have a nice career like Gayle's.

Gayle went on her way. Now she was smiling, too. It had just been a momentary exchange, yet the little glow and sense of sparked connection stayed with her all morning. When one of her subordinates, Jack Farley, came in for his monthly update meeting, Gaye tried a similar experiment with him. She felt Jack perk up when she listened carefully to his answers, and she noticed that he shared more information than he usually did. He even offered some ideas about how she could help him achieve his objectives for the next month. That had never happened before.

Gayle began to feel that she was on to something. She started paying more and more attention to the quality of her interactions with others. Soon this small set of experiments blossomed into a conscious change in the way she approached everyday encounters. Within a couple of months, Gayle's experience at ABLE Consulting fundamentally changed. It was as if her positive encounters with others were nourishing something inside her. She felt her sense of health, vitality, and stamina improve. Not only that, but she could see the heightened energy spread through her unit. Encouraged by Gayle's example, people started offering each other more help. Ideas for new services from her group were openly shared. Meetings became more fun and creative. Gayle's colleagues from other units wanted to know what explained the buzz and heightened sense of activity. Gayle wondered if they would believe her if she told them. She would never have imagined that small moves to make meaningful connections could be so transformative.

Gayle's and Brian's stories illustrate the difference that the quality of connections can make to individuals and organizations. If you reflect on your own experiences, my guess is that you will find similar examples in your own history. And what you know on the basis of experience is borne out by considerable research into the effects of high- and low-quality connections on motivation, learning, commitment, and general well-being. The next section outlines some of that research.

■ Connections and Energy

This book views energy as a renewable resource that contributes to making organizations and the people within them extraordinary. By energy I mean the sense of being eager to act and capable of action. Positive energy is experienced as a form of positive affect, making it a reinforcing experience that people enjoy and seek.[3] Greater energy feels like more enthusiasm and greater zest.[4] Reduced energy feels just the opposite—like a reduced or depleted capacity to act.

Energy is the fuel that makes great organizations run. Chief Executive William L. Robertson of Weston Solutions, a privately held national environment and redevelopment firm, describes the power of energy this way: "Energy can make all the difference between whether you know you are going to have greatness, mediocrity, or failure."[5]

Every interaction with others at work—big or small, short or lengthy—has the potential to create or deplete vital energy. Energizing interactions are high-quality connections. The energy they create is infectious. Where positive energy is activated through a high-quality connection, it can lead to what psychologist Barbara Frederickson calls "positive spirals."[6] The logic of positive spirals goes something like this. People who have high-quality connections experience more energy and more positive emotions such as joy, interest, and love. This state of being increases their capacity to think and act in the moment. In turn, this change builds more capacity and desire to effectively interact with others, generating more opportunities for energy to spread.

Management researchers Rob Cross, Wayne Baker, and their colleagues have been studying the effects of energy in work networks. They note how energy can be renewed and spread as individuals infect each other by connecting in positive ways. One of the managers in their study describes meetings where people are connecting on a real and engaged level that creates a sustained sense of energy: "They are just amazing meetings. People are naturally building off of each other. I am able to think faster and retrieve more for sure. And the ideas themselves, and the way they are forming, just generate a self-reinforcing loop that drives the energy higher and higher."[7]

By the same token, corrosive connections drain vital energy from the organization. Like high-quality connections, they can be infectious. As one manager told me, "Corrosive connections are like black holes: they absorb all of the light in the system and give back nothing in return."

The Damage Done by Corrosive Connections

Exactly how do low- and high-quality connections produce such dramatic effects? Like high-quality connections, corrosive connections can be simple, everyday encounters. They are contacts in which attention, trust, and mutual regard are lacking. It's tempting to shrug off incivility and thoughtlessness as inconsequential, but such connections are not benign. Corrosive connections inflict multiple levels of damage on individuals and organizations that should not be ignored.

Damage to Individuals
Corrosive connections have a number of damaging effects on individuals. To begin with, corrosive connections make it more difficult for employees to do their work. Connections that sap energy turn people inward, both for protection and for sense-making. When people are caught in low-quality connections, they end up doing lots of what psychologists call "motive work," trying to figure out why people are treating them this way. Thus low-quality connections cause distractions that make it difficult for people to engage fully in their tasks. This effect is visible in Brian's story, where the corrosive connection with his boss began to infect and distract other people in his unit. Over time, this type of lower task engagement takes a toll in the quality and efficiency of the work people are able to deliver.

The damage done to people's capacity to do work when dealing with corrosive connections is clearly evident from the effects of incivility in organizations. Uncivil behaviors include being rude and discourteous and displaying a lack of regard for others—all of which are indicators of corrosive connections.[8] Employees who are targets of incivility at work spend an inordinate time worrying about the incident and trying to avoid the person who instigated the uncivil behavior. Not surprisingly, in these kinds of situations people are reluctant to do extra work that goes beyond the strictest job specifications.[9]

Corrosive connections are also a potent force in damaging psychological well-being and inducing stress.[10] In corrosive connections people often have the experience of being devalued and disrespected, eroding feelings of felt worth. Such experiences create a major strain that taxes people's emotional and cognitive capacity to function effectively. For example, Brian found himself getting more and more anxious when he had to interact with the vice president of Finance. The increased anxiety contributed to his fear of giving presentations or even sharing information, making him perform less effectively. The deterioration in his performance further fueled his anxiety and self-focus. The corrosion in the connection sent him spinning in a downward spiral that made it increasingly hard for him to perform well.

Managers can leave major damage in their wake by creating corrosive connections with their subordinates.[11] Often, the source of corrosion is not a major blowup but a series of everyday acts that communicate disrespect or mistrust. In Brian's case, small acts of exclusion and the simple lack of recognition chipped away at his sense of worth and competence. Even worse is being managed with what organizational researcher Blake Ashforth calls "petty tyranny" (using little digs that whittle away at people's sense of self-esteem or punishing people for unexplainable reasons).[12] This kind of management style increases frustration and alienation, and creates a sense of helplessness for subordinates. The result can be anxiety, depression, and emotional exhaustion.[13]

The damage done by corrosive connections at work can also migrate to other domains of people's lives, such as connections with family and with friends. One senior manager told me, "I wish I could turn the clock back to the time that my kids were young. I was under extreme pressure at work and many of my working relationships were absolutely poisonous, yet I felt that I couldn't escape them. What did I do as a result? I brought it all home and tried to 'control' everyone. As a result I made a mess of almost everything, at work and at home. It was a very sad time and it continues to hurt even after many years."

Damage to the Organization

If you hold in mind the costs of corrosive connections on individuals, it is easy to see how corrosive connections undermine an organization's capacity to perform well. Low-quality connections eat away at employees' capability, knowledge, motivation, commitment, and emotional reserves. Moreover, corrosive connections can spark revenge, cheating, and other destructive behaviors.

Corrosive connections also harm organizations because the damage often spreads beyond the initial connection. People cannot help being influenced to some degree by the role models around them, even if they see that a behavior is harmful. For example, in one study of thirty-five work groups in twenty organizations, the antisocial behavior of the group (for example, saying something to purposely hurt another person at work, criticizing people at work, saying rude things) had a strong effect on the antisocial behavior of individuals.[14] As the title of the research article ("Monkey See, Monkey Do") suggests, simply observing the way people treat each other in low-quality connections changes the behavior of the observers, magnifying the corrosive effects.

Corrosion also spreads because people in corrosive connections often take out their pain on others. One manager I know who was in a taxing yet strategically critical staff job explained the dynamic this way: "I have several people I work with where the relationship is really difficult. They come and see me and throw up on me. What do I do with that pain? I often find myself looking for someone else to throw up on."[15]

Clearly, corrosive connections directly impair the effectiveness of the organization in a variety of ways. When you couple these direct costs with the opportunity costs of not having energy-generating, high-quality connections, the performance implications are stunning.

The Benefits Created by High-Quality Connections

The upside of high-quality connections is enormous.[16] The benefits are much greater and more wide-ranging than you might imagine, and they have momentous consequences for both individuals and organizations.

Benefits for Individuals
High-quality connections benefit individuals both in their overall well-being and in their work performance. First, high-quality connections facilitate physical and psychological health.[17] Research suggests that people who have more high-quality interactions during the course of a day register greater well-being, as evidenced by more positive emotions and greater experienced vitality.[18] High-quality connection revitalize, helping people to live longer by reducing the risk of death through strengthening the immune system and lowering blood pressure, reducing stress levels, and arming people with protective factors that make them less susceptible to depression and self-destructive behaviors.[19]

Second, high-quality connections enable individuals to engage more fully in the tasks that compose their jobs.[20] When people are in high-quality connections, they feel a heightened capacity to devote time to and concentrate on the work at hand. Why do high-quality connections have this effect? Some argue it is because they provide a safe psychological haven that gives people freedom to get engaged, to let go and to more fully concentrate on the tasks at hand.[21] Others argue that in high-quality connections one person provides safe emotional space for another, allowing for the expression of natural feelings of confusion, uncertainty, anxiety, and frustration. Expressing such feelings is often essential to letting oneself get fully connected to mastering a task or activity.[22] Finally, network researchers point out that high-quality connections give people access to both emotional resources (such as excitement or support) and instrumental resources (such as information) that allow them to engage in their tasks more effectively.[23]

Third, people learn more easily when they enjoy high-quality connections with others. Being in this form of connection calls up positive emotions like joy, excitement, and interest. Positive emotions expand people's capacity to attend to and think about different types of actions.[24] For example, experiencing joy creates the desire to play, to be creative, and to think outside the box. This emotional response facilitates people's willingness and capacity to learn.[25] People also learn better when in high-quality connections because these kinds of connections create conditions where information is more easily shared and where people can more easily make mistakes and take risks. For example, anthropologist Julian Orr did an in-depth case study of Xerox technical representatives that showed how high-quality connections facilitated the development and sharing of tacit knowledge for fixing copiers. The vitality of the connections between people facilitated storytelling and made asking questions safe. The effect was to enhance both individual learning and the learning of the group.[26] The case of Gayle at the start of this chapter illustrates this kind of effect. As Gayle took time to be present and listened more actively in her meetings with Jack Farley, he shared more information. In turn, Gayle opened up with a wider set of concerns, allowing Jack to participate more fully in decisions that affected both of them. With a more vibrant connection, both people experienced enhanced conditions for learning.

Benefits for the Organization

The organizational benefits of high-quality connections are just as striking as the benefits to individual employees. First, high-quality connections enhance the capacity to cooperate within and across units. Cooperation is a lubricant that makes the everyday work of organizations run smoothly. Cooperation shows up in organizations in all kinds of ways. Sometimes it means staying late and going the extra mile to help a fellow employee. Other times it involves investing time and effort in problem solving or in meeting or exceeding the expectations of a coworker or boss. Whatever form it takes, cooperation implies a loyalty to the relationship over and above loyalty to oneself. When there are high-quality connections between employees and their peers, between employees and their bosses, and in other critical connection points, cooperation is a natural by-product.

Second, high-quality connections facilitate effective coordination between interdependent parts of an organization. For example, the complicated task of producing on-time flight departures for airlines requires enormous coordination between members of cross-functional teams of pilots, flight attendants, gate agents, ticket agents, ramp agents, baggage handlers, operations agents, cabin cleaners, fuelers, mechanics, and freight agents. Management researcher Jody Hoffer Gittell found that the level of problem solving, helping, mutual respect, shared goals, and shared knowledge between employees during the complex delivery of flight departures strongly predicted team performance in terms of both efficiency (gate time per departure and staff time per passenger) and quality (customer complaints, baggage handling, and late arrivals).[27] In the airlines that maintained high-quality connections, employees readily adapted their work to help each other out to make performance goals.

People felt a strong sense of mutuality; if one person worked hard to accommodate an overburdened ticket agent, the helper could count on the agent to help out in a future crunch time. Gittell's study provides compelling evidence that the quality of the relationships between people facilitates complex coordination as individuals work effectively together to improvise and adapt in order to deliver a complete service performance.[28]

Third, high-quality connections strengthen employees' attachments to their work organizations. It should come as no surprise that where employees enjoy positive connections with others at work, their intention to stay at the organization strengthens.[29] High-quality connections function like relational anchors, mooring and stabilizing people's sense of attachment to their work organization. A vice president of marketing in a large cosmetic manufacturer told me that she put up with salary inequities, infrequent raises, and frustration with the firm's relative slowness of competitive response because of the quality of her connections with other employees: "It is not fake, it is real. I can count on them to be there if life turns sour or things get rough. This feeling is something that money can't buy." Another manager told me about his department's weekly intake meeting of new consulting work: "At some times of the year, we are very busy and find it difficult to take on new projects, but when we ask whether people can help each other with questions or problems with their current projects, it is amazing to hear them say that of course they can help. Our staff meetings have become a place where people receive expressions of support and help from others. Members of the team know that they can come to the meetings and receive the energy and help of others."

Fourth, high-quality connections can facilitate the transmission of purpose, a key consideration for organizations that rely on culture and the transmission of values as a means to build loyalty and assure competitive success. High-quality connections between employees, and between employees and customers, create a type of high-speed, rich conductivity that sustains an organization's culture and strengthens employees' commitment. For example, at Charles Schwab Inc., management relies extensively on the transmission and diffusion of stories that concretely illustrate its core values of fairness, empathy, responsiveness, and service, thereby deepening employees' commitment to these values.[30] Without mutuality and energy in the connections between people at Schwab, the infectiousness of the culture would be minimized.

Fifth, high-quality connections encourage dialogue and deliberation and thereby facilitate organizational learning. Connections are the repository for social knowledge about how to get things done.[31] They are major conduits by which managers learn about their organization's capabilities relative to other firms.[32] Connections are also the medium that creates communities of practice where people learn and achieve competence.[33] High-quality connections create the social fabric that supports ongoing learning processes.

Finally, an organization's capacity to adapt and change is tied to the quality of the relationships between organizational members. Arguments for this link come from people applying ideas from the science of complexity to the understanding of organizational effectiveness.[34] Consultants Roger Lewin and Birute Regine make the link this way: "In complex adaptive systems, how we interact and the kinds of relationships we form has everything to do with what kind of culture emerges, and this in turn, has everything to do with the emergence of creativity, productivity, and innovation."[35] According to this perspective, what these consultants call "care-full relationships" between people are key to innovation and change. *Care-full* (high-quality) connections ensure richer, more frequent communication between people. They motivate people to do their best. They allow people to take risks for the good of the whole. In short, high-quality connections are the foundation for adaptive change.

■ Structure of the Book: Building and Sustaining High-Quality Connections

Given the costs of corrosive connections and the benefits of high-quality connections for both organizations and individuals, it follows that paying attention to the quality of connections should be a top priority for any manager. This book is designed to assist managers by addressing three core questions:

- How do I build high-quality connections in my work organization?
- How do I help myself and others deal with corrosive, low-quality connections?
- How can I design or select organizational contexts that are conducive to building and sustaining high-quality connections?

The answers to these three questions form the structure of the book. Figure 1.1 shows a simple model of the book's core arguments.

Chapters Two through Four develop the core idea that high-quality connections are created in everyday interactions with others. They outline a range of strategies for energizing your workplace, organized in terms of three main pathways to high-quality connection: respectful engagement, task enabling, and trusting. Each chapter explains the essence of a particular pathway, enumerates several strategies, describes and illustrates specific behaviors for deploying these strategies, and considers the challenges you might face, together with some starting points for overcoming them.

Chapter Two focuses on strategies of *respectful engagement*—how to engage others in ways that send messages of value and worth. I describe five major strategies for creating respectful engagement: being present, being genuine, communicating affir-

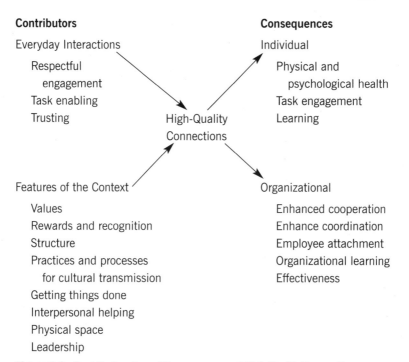

Figure 1.1. Contributors to and Consequences of High-Quality Connections

mation, effective listening, and supportive communication. Being present can take multiple forms, including minimizing distraction, using appropriate body language, and being available. Being genuine involves acting from authentic feelings and motivations. Communicating affirmation can be achieved by looking for the value in another person, communicating recognition, expressing genuine interest, and treating time as precious. Effective listening involves both empathy and active listening. Finally, supportive communication can be achieved by making requests rather than demands, communicating in specific rather than general terms, and making descriptive rather than evaluative statements.

Chapter Three zeroes in on *task enabling*—ways of interacting that facilitate another person's successful performance.

Again, five strategies are discussed: teaching, designing, advocating, accommodating, and nurturing. Teaching involves the sharing of useful knowledge, insight, and information. Designing involves structuring features of a job to facilitate another's performance. Advocating involves actively helping another navigate the political landscape of the organization. Accommodating involves being flexible in ways that enable others to perform better. Finally, nurturing involves facilitating others' success by addressing their developmental needs.

Chapter Four focuses on *building trust*—acting in ways that convey to others the belief that they will act with integrity, dependability, and benevolence. You build high-quality connections through trusting by what you say (for example, by sharing valuable information about yourself), by what you don't say (not accusing another person of bad intent), by what you do (sharing responsibility) and by what you do not do (not using surveillance or monitoring to check up on someone else's behavior).

Chapter Five changes direction and faces squarely the issue of how to deal constructively with corrosive connections. The chapter describes a range of strategies, including bounding and buffering (minimizing the damage), buttressing and strengthening (increasing your capacity to deal with corrosive connections and derive strength from them), and targeting and transforming (changing the connection itself). These strategies can help you and the people you manage consider a fuller range of possibilities for reducing the cost of these harmful relationships at work.

Chapter Six, the final chapter of the book, moves the discussion from individual interactions to the features of organizations that enable or disable the building of high-quality connections. Simply said, some organizations are highly conducive to building high-quality connections and others are not. How do you as a manager think about building a context that enables these generative connections? Chapter Six addresses this question by presenting seven key clues for identifying contexts that enable high-quality connections: values, practices for rewards and recognition, structure, practices and procedures for getting things done, norms for interpersonal helping, the design of physical space, and the behavior of leaders. Each clue suggests strategies you can deploy as you work to improve the climate for high-quality connections in your own work group, department, unit, or organization.

Each chapter in this book concludes with assessments and other tools for putting the ideas into practice. I've designed the assessments to help spotlight areas of connecting that are working well and areas that may be in need of repair. You can use these insights both to improve your own connecting practices and to enhance the connecting strategies of the people you manage.

■ An Invitation

Let me conclude this introductory chapter by inviting you to engage seriously in exploring how you can energize your workplace by building and sustaining high-quality connections. In work, and in life generally, more generative possibilities appear to people who believe they can understand and make a difference in their own situation and the situation of others. This book is all about helping you see new possibilities for bringing greater energy and vitality to your own life, and the lives of people you work with, by managing in a way that reduces corrosive connections and increases high-quality connections. I hope the book gives you a heightened sense of understanding and a strengthened belief that you can in fact make big differences with even small changes in the actions you take each and every day.

CHAPTER SUMMARY

In this chapter I have introduced the core idea that effective leadership and management requires building and sustaining high-quality connections for yourself and for others. High-quality connections are ties between people that are marked by mutual regard, trust, and active engagement. They can happen in an instant, and they infuse both people with a sense of vitality and energy. These kinds of connections are life-giving. Unfortunately, too often organizational involves just the opposite—low-quality or corrosive connections that diminish people's sense of worth and drain them of energy.

The quality of connections has a profound effect on both individuals and organizations. Corrosive connections diminish employees' capacity to get their work done well and can damage their health. The toll on individuals can severely impair organizational effectiveness, especially since the corrosion often spreads across the organization. In contrast, high-quality connections enhance psychological and physical health, facilitate task engagement, and enable learning. At the organization level, they facilitate cooperation and effective coordination, increase employee attachment, help transmit organizational culture, and enable organizational learning and adaptation.

This book describes three pathways to building high-quality connections: respectful engagement, task enabling, and trusting. It also offers strategies for dealing with corrosive connections. Finally, it suggests ways to create an organizational context that is conducive to building and sustaining high-quality connections. My hope is that it will both inspire and equip you to take the small steps that can make a major difference in your life and the life of your organization.

Respectful Engagement

You've sweated to prepare for the monthly project team meeting. Late nights. Lots of coffee. You've checked the assumptions and the numbers multiple times. Your report is important to the whole team, and you can't help feeling a few butterflies as you wait for the meeting to begin.

Your boss comes in and sits down, acknowledging your presence only with a distracted nod. It's almost as if he is looking right through you. Seemingly preoccupied with other thoughts, he asks you to start your presentation. While you're talking, he barely makes eye contact. After you're done, his only response is a perfunctory "Nice job." You are not at all sure he means it.

Sound familiar? Encounters like this one are all too common, and they are more than just unpleasant. Experiences of disrespectful engagement or nonengagement deplete you, eating away at the reserve of motivation, commitment, and openness that you bring to the table.

Contrast this experience with the kinds of encounters you might have with Justine Calfone, manager of new product development in a pharmaceutical division known for its consistent flow of newly patented products and for its ability to retain top-flight scientists despite alluring offers from competitors. Justine also has monthly project review meetings, but the minute she enters the room, her affirmative comments, eye contact, and body language send you clear messages that she is glad you are there and is genuinely interested in what you have to say. Her comments and questions are always discerning and tough. If she disagrees with the facts or with your conclusions, she is clear to specify what she has heard, what her interpretations are, and how she has reached a different conclusion. She invites differences of opinion as long as they are offered constructively. She remains issue focused and specific, always making clear that she has listened to the various opinions in the room. Believe it or not, people look forward to her project review meetings for the sense of accomplishment and excitement that they generate.

Justine's techniques exemplify the first pathway to building high-quality connections, respectful engagement. Respectful engagement means being present to others, affirming them, and communicating and listening in a way that manifests regard and an appreciation of the other's worth. It doesn't have to be a deep encounter. It can happen in the hallway in route to a meeting. It can happen on the phone lines in a customer-calling center. Small acts of respectful engagement infuse a relationship with greater energy while at the same time sending signals and modeling behavior that gets picked up by others.

At the level of the firm, Justine serves as a reminder that respectful engagement builds loyalty. It enables effective performance by facilitating work coordination and enhancing the speed and quality of learning. You hear the transforming power of respectful engagement when people at work say they have had their "battery charged" or their "energy renewed" after a meeting or an interaction with a colleague. The infusion of "juice" shows up in the way people feel more vibrant and engaged, better able to focus and learn. And the energy charge spreads. By recharging people, small acts of respectful engagement spread positive currents beyond the initial point of contact.

In this chapter, I'll first take a closer look at what respectful engagement is and how it contributes to high-quality connections. I'll then consider the behaviors that create respectful engagement, some challenges you may face in putting these behaviors into practice, and practical steps you can take to begin traveling this pathway.

■ The Power of Respectful Engagement

Everyone needs respectful engagement with others, but in many work organizations, few get it. For many people, and for many organizations, disrespectful engagement is the norm rather than the exception. The extent of incivility or disrespectful engagement in the workplace is disturbing:[1]

- 90 percent of respondents in one poll believed that incivility is a serious problem and that it contributes to violence and erodes moral values.
- In another poll, three out of four respondents believed that incivility is getting worse.
- More than half of the 327 front-line workers surveyed in another poll indicated that they had experienced acts of mistreatment at work during the past three years.

- One third of more than 600 nurses surveyed experienced verbal abuse during their previous five days of work.[2]

The sting of disrespect may be felt most acutely when it comes from a current or future boss, or from someone else above you in the hierarchy. Often the telltale signs that a particular person or the firm as a whole is not a good place for energy-creating connections show up the moment you cross over the firm's boundaries as a temporary or permanent employee. An incident recounted in the *Wall Street Journal* is all too typical: "The day he hired on, his assigned mentor showed him his office and walked away without a word—no tour of the office, no introductions to co-workers, 'in short, no information,' the consultant says. Later, in a meeting, a partner treated him like a piece of furniture. Pointing him out as a new hire, the partner said, 'I don't know if he's any good. Somebody try him out and let me know.'"[3]

Our bodies and our minds are well-tuned sensors that pick up the signals that another person sends about our basic worth. Nonverbal and verbal cues are jam-packed with meaning in affirming or disconfirming worth and value. The example that began this chapter or the incident described in the *Wall Street Journal* may well have registered in your body, even though you were reading about remote events. If it is happening to you right now, the physical effects of energy depletion are even more pronounced. There is that churn in the stomach when you are speaking to someone and it is clear that they are not listening. There is that slight blow to the belly when someone makes small moves like turning away, working on other tasks, or tightly folding his arms. The depletion of energy from disrespectful engagement reduces your willingness to go the extra mile, to take risks, or seek out the other person's needs. Multiply this energy-depleting effect many times over and you can see how small instances of disrespectful engagement can sap the spirit of an entire work unit or organization.

Contrast this destructive power of disrespectful engagement with the energizing power of interactions that communicate regard, that affirm your worth. A colleague sends you an e-mail note just to express appreciation for a contribution you made at a meeting. Someone from corporate headquarters, whom you've met only casually, not only remembers your name but asks with genuine interest how your son-in-law is faring in school. A customer actively seeks information from you in way that makes clear she really wants to know your take on an issue. Although small acts on their own, these interactions have a cumulative effect that goes far beyond your momentary flush of pleasure. When another person engages you in ways that honor your existence and value, at least two important things happen. First, your self-esteem is elevated. Second, you are drawn closer to the person who is affirming you. The connective tissue between the two of you becomes stronger, more vibrant, more resilient.

These effects are related to each other and mutually reinforcing. Many years ago a sociologist named Charles Cooley coined the phrase "the looking glass self" as a way to say that our own sense of worth is tied to how others engage or interact with us. According to this view, the self we create is dependent on how others mirror back to us who we are. When others engage us respectfully, they reflect an image that is positive and valued. They create a sense of social dignity that confirms our worth and even our sense of competence.[4] In so doing, they help us to create a secure basis for seeking out connection to others. Respectful engagement thus empowers and energizes us, creating a heightened sense of our capacity to act both in relation to other people and with respect to ourselves.[5] By the same token, acts of disrespectful engagement reflect an image of a person who is of limited value and worth. Not only do they sap our self-confidence, they encourage us to withdraw and withhold, moving away from rather than connecting with other people.

Respectful engagement creates high-quality connection and high-quality connection creates respectful engagement. It is a powerful virtuous circle. And like stones tossed into a pond, acts of respectful engagement can have ripple effects that spread throughout a work unit or an organization. Thus Justine Calfone's subordinates are changed and inspired by experiencing the effects of respectful engagement from their boss. They probably act in a similar fashion toward her, completing the circle of respect. If they learn from Justine's example, their efforts to engage others in a respectful way are likely to elicit a similar response from those they work with, forming a solid foundation for high-quality connections well beyond Justine's immediate circle.

■ How to Create Respectful Engagement

Given the energizing and connective power of respectful engagement, how do you create this power by the way you interact with others? This section offers five major strategies for using respectful engagement to build high-quality connections. Three of the strategies "till the ground" for engaging someone in a more active way in conversations that are respectful: *conveying presence, being genuine,* and *communicating affirmation.* These ways of being with another person are foundations for the more active processes of *effective listening* and *supportive communication.*

Conveying Presence

How many times have you heard a colleague, a customer, or a friend recall the power of your "just being there"? Of course, they meant something more than just the fact of your physical presence. They meant you were there for them, openly and attentively. Each time you come into contact with another person (virtually or in real time), you have a chance to be present or not psychologically. Presence is a foundation state for respectful engagement. Without it, none of the other strategies for engagement will work.

Being present with another person implies being psychologically available and receptive. It means creating a sense of being open and subject to being changed through the connection with that person. Presence is a gift that one person gives another. Martin Buber, a wise philosopher of connection, put it this way: "In spite of all similarities, every living situation has, like a newborn child, a new face, that has never been before and will never come again. It demands of you a reaction, which cannot be prepared beforehand. It demands nothing of what is past. It demands presence, responsibility. It demands you."[6]

Conveying presence means turning one's attention to another. Attention is a precious commodity in organizations of all types. It is easily consumed, deflected, or distracted. Communicating presence is as much about resisting distraction as it is about inviting engagement. Think of the mound of distractions in your current office setting: computers, phones, fax machines, piled paper, to-do lists. Any one of these can deflect you from being present to another. When two people at work deliberately direct attention toward each other and away from other possible distractions, they activate a sense of mutual connection that energizes both people. In the words of Edward Hallowell, "A five-minute conversation can make all the difference in the world if the parties participate actively. To make it work, you have to set aside what you're doing, put down the memo you were reading, disengage from your laptop, abandon your daydream and bring your attention to bear upon the person you are with. Usually, when you do this, the other person (or people) will feel the energy and respond in kind, naturally."[7]

Making contact, human to human, does not require conversation. Yet even in conversation, the charge that one gets comes from the contact. As communication theorist Joost Meerloo put it, "The delight in conversation comes not from making sense but from making contact."[8] Here are some of the ways you can make contact by conveying presence:

Conveying Presence Through Body Language
Human bodies provide rich displays of how we feel and what we believe about another person. More than 50 percent of the impact of a message is conveyed by body movements, 38 percent by tone of voice (volume, pitch, and the like), and only 7 percent by words.[9] While the meaning of body movements and facial expressions depends on the situation, several body moves frequently convey a sense of "being there" for another person. Physical gestures like eye contact or hand movements can display whether or not someone is on track for another. Here is one version of advice about how to use body language to convey presence: "Instead of allowing your body message to alienate, use it to convey caring. Begin by keeping still. Focus your eyes on the speaker's eyes, glancing away occasionally so that your gaze does not feel invasive. (Direct looking increases intimacy.) You can still appear bored if your expression is glazed. So make looking an active process. Unknit your brow. Relax your jaw. Uncross your arms. Lean slightly forward."[10]

Thus, as a step toward respectful engagement, pay attention to the signals that your body sends regarding your readiness and willingness to be open and engaged with another person.

Conveying Presence By Being Available
Availability is another way to signal presence: being at hand, being ready, and being capable of being used. You communicate this state of being by how you respond to requests from others for time, for attention, or for physical presence.

Sarah Wallace, a very busy marketing executive who often has people at her doorstep giving her quick synopses of rapidly changing events, is an expert at signaling availability effectively. The people who stop by are often hesitant to interrupt for more extended periods. If she senses that someone is deeply troubled, her face will signal her recognition of, and empathy with, the person's distress. She will extend her arms with the palms up and gesture the person into her office, while saying something like, "This sounds very troubling to you and so it's important to me that we talk now." She leaves no doubt in people's minds that they are important and that she is available for connection.

Conveying presence means being focused on the here and now as opposed to the past or the future. This focus is tough to maintain in work organizations, with constant pressure to look forward to future goals, future commitments, and future actions. Sometimes it takes explicit gestures and actions to remind yourself (and the person you are interacting with) that you are present and you are focused on this very moment. I know when I am meeting with students, if the phone rings, I explicitly unplug it in their presence to signal I am there—now—for them. My former adviser used to make his availability known by clearing off his desk and getting me a glass of water, signaling that he was available for a block of time and was welcoming me to engage now.

Being Genuine

Respectful engagement also means removing fronts and speaking and reacting from a real and honest place. Of course, this is always easier said than done. None of us are very good at knowing exactly when and how we are genuine. However, our "authenticity detectors" are often good at reading when we are disingenuous or putting on a front.[11] We sense that our behavior feels fake, even a bit deceitful, but also safe. But our feeling of safety comes at a price. The absence of genuineness blocks our capacity to respectfully engage another person. Respectful engagement requires being real.

Being genuine often means behaving toward someone based on internal desires and motivations as opposed to external pressures and force. For example, if someone acts toward me in a kind and caring manner and I think it is because of what they actually feel (as opposed to the context telling them they "have to be kind and caring"), I am more likely to believe the connection is sustainable. By contrast, a local hospital recently undermined its staff's mutual connections by implementing what it calls the "5-feet 10-feet rule": it now requires all employees to smile at anyone else in the hospital who comes within ten feet of them and to say hello to those within five feet. One unintended consequence of this rule is likely to be that people who know of it will regard the smiles or acknowledgments they receive as mandatory and therefore false.

Communicating Affirmation

Communicating affirmation is critical for tilling the soil for connection. Communicating affirmation means going beyond being present. It means actively looking for the positive core or the "divine spark in another."[12] Communicating affirmatively is accomplished in multiple ways. Each affirmative gesture adds to the potential for a high-quality connection.

Affirming Someone's Situation
One way to communicate affirmation is by recognizing and understanding another person's situation. For example, simple statements offered when you sense that someone is under extreme pressure at work can express affirmation and open the door for connection. A senior manager of a consulting firm told me a story about an especially rough time when his unit was receiving company-wide heat for budget shortfalls that were out of the unit's control. He recalled his manager saying, "I also

want you to know that I've been watching you and *no one* could do this job better than you are doing it!" Upon hearing these words, despite being known as a hard-boiled executive, he actually broke down and cried because he thought that no one was noticing his struggle.

Looking for the Value in the Other
It also conveys affirmation to imagine and see others in a positive light. Actively looking for the value in another means actively approaching another person with the expectation of affirming who they are and what they have to offer. In *The Art of Possibility*, Zander and Zander call this move one of "Giving the other person an A." As they describe it, this type of practice and attitude is transformative: "It is a shift in attitude that makes it possible for you to speak freely about your own thoughts and feeling, while at the same time, you support others to be all they dream of being. The practice of giving an A transports your relationships from the world of measurement into the universe of possibility."[13]

People who do business negotiation for a living work on a similar logic. They advise participants to "think of the person you are negotiating with not as an opponent, but as someone who can illuminate the situation and might have insights that are radically different than your own."[14] This first move sets in motion a process that often creates more sharing of real information and interests, as well as more integrative solutions.

An affirmative stance means engaging the process by giving someone the benefit of the doubt. The impact of this stance was clearly evident in the approach taken by Justine at the start of this chapter. This kind of positive view of the other lays the groundwork for quality connections by "lowering the costs of communication by explicitly expressing the value you place on the other person's perspective."[15]

Expressing Recognition

Conveying affirmation is also accomplished through what you say and how you say it. Organizations offer endless opportunities to affirm others in ways that are genuine and transformative. Watch Marty Johns, head of product development at an Internet start-up, use a project team's first meeting to create fertile ground for connection by the way he introduces the team members to each other:

Marty Johns has assembled a prize team—people handpicked for their probable contributions to the next generation of new products—for this very successful start. Although the reputations of the people assembled precede them, the team has never been face-to-face in a room. The air is full of excitement, with everyone anticipating the stretch goals and high standards involved in this new assignment. Marty begins the meeting in an unusual way. Rather than having the members introduce themselves, he begins with an appreciative introduction of each one, offering his take on the unique talents, perspectives, and qualities of each chosen team member as a human being. The introductions are not long, but each adjective and example Marty offers seems compelling and heartfelt. The descriptions name what Marty loves and appreciates in each person. Each person being introduced is visibly embarrassed at the description, but inspired and thankful to be on the team as they learn of the positive qualities of their team members. The introductions take twenty minutes total, but the soil for growth of the team has been tilled with respect and positive regard. In this simple act Marty has taken an ordinary routine used in a first meeting of strangers and turned it into an extraordinary opportunity for constructive connection. The energy in the room at the introductions' end is palpable.

Expressed recognition serves to recognize a job well done or a contribution someone has made, but more than that, it affirms the value of the person to whom it is offered. Effective leaders realize the affirming power of expressed recognition, and they devote valued time to its delivery. One of my favorite examples of this form of affirmative leadership is demonstrated by John Chambers, CEO of Cisco Systems. A frequent activity for Chambers involves early breakfast meetings with groups of employees. The meetings give employees a chance to ask Chambers questions, but they also give him an opportunity to express his recognition of the contributions of each employee. The practice of continuous recognition is further institutionalized by the policy that enables on-the-spot bonuses. "With prior approval from the boss anybody can give anyone an on-the-spot bonus ranging from a free dinner to as much as $5000 for going the extra mile—and these can be approved within 24 hours."[16]

However, affirmations are not just bold strokes by inspired leaders or creative personnel strategies for recognition. They are human linkages we can forge with others every day if we choose. Mary, a project director at a high-impact research center, reported the positive feedback she received from an affirmative interaction with another staff person: "One day last year I called the Financial Operations coordinator to ask for some help in instructions about writing a report. He was very kind, looked into the situation, and resolved it for me. I was very appreciative so I called him just to say thanks. Well, he couldn't believe that that was the only reason I was calling. I told him I just wanted to acknowledge his efforts. He told me that if I ever needed anything from him again not to hesitate to call."

Despite the power of recognition and affirmation as a basis of building connection, the evidence is that most people do not get much of it. In one study, just under half of North American workers said they did not receive any recognition for a job well done. Further, a similar percentage report they never get recognized for outstanding performance.[17] This study's bottom line is that most people in work organizations are starved for recognition. The scarcity of this kind of affirmation makes it an even more powerful route for building connection.

Expressions of Genuine Interest

Beyond recognition, you can affirm others when you convey that you are genuinely interested in their feelings, thoughts, or actions. Expressions of genuine interest are part of conveying "appreciation of the wholeness of the other person."[18] Expressions of interest show up in all kinds of work interactions. For example, ritualistic greetings such as "How are you?" vary considerably in how much genuine interest in another person they express. One of my favorite examples of expressed genuine interest was told to me by Tim Pollack, a former MBA student, who went to work for a Wall Street firm. He was shocked to see how much time his new boss spent finding out what people in his unit cared about. In a week's time, his new boss had learned what hobbies he liked, details of his family, even some of his favorite foods. He learned these details through incidental questions and gentle probes that Tim experienced as ways his boss came to know him as a unique individual.

Respectful engagement and genuine interest can build a connective wisdom that boosts organization-level competencies. This point was dramatically illustrated in the immediate aftermath of the terrorist attack on the United States on September 11, 2001. David Stark and John Kelly studied the recovery efforts of firms in New York City, trying to understand how the firms' capabilities allowed them to achieve quick technical recovery. They told a moving story of one World Trade Center senior IT executive who explained his firm's ability to resume trading on the bond market despite major loss of technical support and human lives:

> We had 47 hours to get [ready for] September 13th, when the bond markets reopened and there was one situation that our

technology department had that they spent more time on than anything else. It was getting into the systems, [figuring out] the IDs of the systems because so many people had died and the people that knew how to get into those systems and who knew the backup . . . and the second emergency guy were all gone. How did they get into those systems? They sat around the group, they [technology officers] talked about where they went on vacation, what their kids' names were, what their wives' names were, what their dogs' names were, you know, every imaginable thing about their personal life. And the fact that we knew things about their personal life to break into those IDs and into the systems to be able to get the technology up and running before the bond market opened, I think [that] is probably the number one connection between technology, communication, and people.[19]

Leaders have numerous planned and unplanned events and opportunities to genuinely convey interest in other people. Perhaps needless to say, expressions of interest must be authentic to build connection. People have finely tuned "sincerity detectors" when it comes to expressions of interest in them as individuals.

Inauthenticity wastes energy at the same time that it prevents connection. Bob Shapiro, former CEO of Monsanto, suggests that "inauthenticity diverts energy and makes us tired at the end of the day. So it's an efficiency as well as a mental health issue."[20] In contrast, when someone genuinely wants to know who you are—what you care about, what "makes you tick"— the expression of interest begins the cycle of positive growth that typifies high-quality connections.

One leader whom employees consistently see as genuinely interested in their uniqueness, their personal welfare, and the welfare of the organization is Hatim Tyabji, former CEO of Veri-Fone. Hatim describes his commitment to genuinely knowing the people who work for and with him in these terms: "You're dealing with human beings that by definition are extremely complex. We all have our strengths, our weaknesses, our insecurities, our egos. The real key is to take a deep interest in people. And try to do your best to understand what their insecurities may be and then work for them. When you reach out to them, they will reach right back. I think that is tremendous. Some say, 'Hatim, big deal. That's common sense.' That's true. The issue is practicing it. The most profound truths in the world are the simplest. Except they don't get practiced."[21]

Conveying interest is not a one-way street. In the dance of connection it is often important to take the first step yourself. Being open, revealing yourself, allowing yourself to be vulnerable are often helpful preludes to engaging someone respectfully. As the director of support services at a local consulting organization told me, not making yourself known in this way can lead to painful consequences:

> Everyone knew that I was on the way up in my career, and I
> thought that I had to be perfect in every way to advance. Perfect work, a perfect home life with a loving spouse, perfect
> health, you get the picture. But at one point, things were far
> from perfect, my spouse and I separated and I began having a
> variety of health problems which affected my work. My first
> reaction was to hide them from everyone at work since I was
> afraid that others would see them as signs of weakness. However, in retrospect, I think that was the wrong thing to do. I
> was hurting terribly at that point in my life and I did not feel
> genuine coming to work and putting on a front that suggested
> everything was fine. It just added more pressure to what was
> already a very difficult time. So I decided to tell a few people
> who were close colleagues. They could not have been more
> supportive, and their support helped me pull myself together
> in that one domain of my life, which helped me as I faced the
> other challenges. I will never forget what they did for me. It
> also helped me realize that many other people face even more

challenging problems than I did, and I now try to reach out to them in a respectful way to show them that I care, just as others cared for me.

The Treatment of Time

The way that you treat others' time is an instant message of respect (or its opposite). On how many occasions have you hustled to get to a meeting on time and learned that no one else did the same? Time is scarce currency in most organizations. It shows you value another person's time if you treat it as precious and rare. Showing up on time, granting time, apologizing for wasting time and respectfully asking for time are small acts that convey affirmation. It's easy to imagine the different feelings conveyed by these two statements: "We need to talk and we need to talk right this minute," versus "I know you're busy, but do you have fifteen minutes for an important short conversation?"

Effective Listening

Really listening to what someone has to say is a form of respectful engagement. But effective listening requires effort. Distractions are the norm in most work settings. The cost is a tuning out, a lack of focus on what someone else is saying and feeling, and a lost opportunity to respectfully engage.

Even when other distractions are not claiming our attention, it takes work to listen effectively. While people can comprehend an average of 600 spoken words per minute, speech usually flows at 100–150 words per minute. The gap is one of the reasons people at work have a hard time listening. Their minds search for other things to keep them busy.[22] In addition, too often the listener focuses on goals for the interaction as opposed to listening to the other person. They listen only partially tuned in, waiting for their own opportunity to speak and therefore never fully attending to what the other person is saying.

Listening that engages another respectfully has two features: it is empathetic and it is active. Empathetic listening is other-centered. It involves putting yourself into another person's shoes, intellectually and emotionally. It starts with a realization that we do not know all that we need to know about another person. It is our job in listening to learn as much as we can about the other's perspective by actively attending to all the cues conveyed by their words and by their actions.

Taking the trouble to understand another's perspective "from the inside out" has real payoff in terms of creating and sustaining high-quality relationships both within and across work organizations. For example, Michele Williams, a faculty member at MIT, completed a study of perspective taking by managerial consultants and found that it both improved the quality of connections with clients and increased clients' evaluations of consultant performance, a key component of consultants' success in securing repeat business.[23]

Two concrete actions will help anyone who wants to be a more empathetic listener at work. First, empathetic listeners *acknowledge the feelings* conveyed explicitly or implicitly in the communication by the other person. "I hear what you are saying." "Your boss's actions must have made you feel belittled and angry." Second, empathetic listeners *try to more fully understand the context* of the person who is speaking, the particular and concrete details of the person's situation. Physicians note the importance of understanding a patient's context as central to knowing what a patient's illness might be and what actions might be helpful to take.[24] Similarly, it is useful to listen empathetically to the circumstances of colleagues at work to better diagnose what kinds of actions will be most effective in a particular situation.

The second part of effective listening involves being active. By *active* I mean being responsive as a listener so as to encourage further communication. Active listening can take many forms. Most important is taking measures while listening that ensure that you are hearing and understanding what someone is saying. This is one of the approaches Justine Calfone uses to create a positive atmosphere for her team.

The active part of listening can be done in many ways. Here is a sampling of possibilities that can be used at times you believe are most fitting:

- *Paraphrasing,* or expressing in your own words what you just heard someone say. "So, let me make sure I am hearing you correctly. When you say that it's a stretch to meet this month's objectives, are you saying you will need more financial resources to meet the objective this month?"
- *Summarizing,* or trying to pull together the ideas and feelings that someone just related. "So if I boil down your last three points, I hear you urging our division to be more aggressive with Supplier X in securing inputs on a timely basis."
- *Clarifying,* or asking questions and inquiring to ensure that you understand the full picture or the points and meaning that the other person is trying to convey. "Correct me if I'm not hearing you right, but I think you are saying—"
- *Soliciting feedback* about how the other person thinks you are doing as a listener. "Do you get the sense that I'm listening to you, that I'm hearing what you have to say?"

In each example the listener leaves space and a comfort zone for the speaker to express that the listening is not working. This gives room for either person to take corrective action to ensure that the speaker feels accurately heard.

Supportive Communication

Respectful engagement also depends on how we communicate—what we say, how we say it and how our communication is understood by the other person. Effective communication marks the

beginning of respectful engagement in which both people produce something that is unique. Through joint openness and presence, the communication creates a fluidity and responsiveness
that contributes to a higher-quality connection. This form of communication does not imply that the speaker knows all the answers; instead, it suggests some humility and invites a dialogue.

More specifically, supportive communication means expressing yourself in a way that allows the other person to hear
you. It means being careful to express views and opinions in
ways that minimize defensiveness on the part of others and
maximizes their clarity about where you stand and how they
can constructively respond.

By contrast, several forms of communication signal an unsupportive attitude: sarcasm, negative comparisons, threats, drag-
ging up the past, framing discussions and outputs of discussions
as win-lose interactions.[25] All these forms of communication hinder the other person's ability to tune in to and understand your
message.

It's useful to explore the difference between supportive and
unsupportive communication, as it highlights the features that
help you communicate in a supportive way. Here are three important guidelines:

Make Requests Rather Than Demands
Communications at work often involve needing to get tasks
done, work assigned, performance reviewed, and deadlines met.
The way that these needs are expressed determines the quality
of connection. In particular, *supportive communications involve requests and not demands.*[26]

The difference between requests and demands is fundamental. It changes the tone, feel, and outcome of any engagement
with another person. We make demands when we send the message that blame or punishment will follow not responding to the
request. Marshall Rosenberg, a management consultant who stud-

ied with Carl Rogers and has become an expert on what he calls "nonviolent communication," gives us surefire signs that we are thinking in terms of demands and not requests: "He should have done that," "They are supposed to do what I ask," or "I have a right to say this."[27] These types of phrases indicate a demand frame of mind because they suggest the intent to judge others' actions based on whether or not they comply. As Rosenberg says, "Once you hear demands, your options are submission or rebellion."[28]

So how do you think in terms of requests and not demands? Rosenberg offers several suggestions. First, *define your objective* when making requests. Requests only work if you genuinely believe that the other person can freely choose a response. Second, *use positive action language.* Rather than suggesting what you don't want (for example, "I don't need you to check with me so often about the project schedule"), express requests in terms of positive actions ("I want you to check with me on a regular weekly basis about the project schedule"). Third, *make requests in the most specific terms possible,* avoiding all the hazards of misinterpretation that accompany vague or ambiguous requests. For example, "I need updates from you on a weekly basis regarding sales projections" is much more effective than "Be sure to keep me updated."

You might be thinking as you read these suggestions, that making requests and not demands violates basic tenets of management. After all, dominant views of the managerial role imply that having influence through making things happen requires demands and not requests. The point here is that this form of communication (and influence) comes at a cost. Demands may get something done in the short run and demonstrate you have power in the moment, but they dilute the connective potential in your relationship. By using genuine requests, you not only do not incur this cost, you invest in a higher-quality connection with the other person, yielding future benefits such as greater trust and more flexibility.

Make Communications Specific

The idea of being specific requests is an instance of a more general recommendation for how to be supportive in communication.[29] Too often communications are couched in vague or global terms. More specific statements carry more information about what the speaker means and provide clearer guidance about what the consequences of action might be. For example, in giving feedback to someone you manage, try to share specific examples of the behavior they exhibited that met or exceeded standards you were looking for. This type of specificity helps a subordinate or peer both understand and accept what you are saying.

Remain Descriptive and Avoid Evaluative Language

Evaluative judgments seep very easily into communications and undermine the possibility of respectful engagement. Like the temptation to make demands rather than requests, the tendency to use judgmental language is a particular hazard for managers. But especially when the judgment is negative, such language only invites a defensive response. The beauty of descriptive as opposed to evaluative communication is that it minimizes defensiveness and conveys helpful, practical information that allows two people to coordinate and move forward on their efforts.

Dave Whetten and Kim Cameron, two experts on managerial skills, say that descriptive communication involves three steps.[30] First, *stay descriptive about the behavior or event* that is the focus of the conversation. Avoid evaluative labels that imply subjective impressions. Whetten and Cameron provide this example of a concrete statement: "Three clients have complained to me this month that you have not responded to their requests."[31] This is a descriptive statement of fact that opens up the possibility of dialogue about the area of concern. In contrast, a statement like "You need to shape up in responding to customer requests" expresses a prejudgment. It implies disrespect for the other person's perspective and invites a defensive response.

Second, *describe the outcomes or reactions associated with the behavior.* It is important to stay focused on the consequences associated with the behavior and not lapse into a discussion of motives or attributions about causes. So, for instance, rather than simply mentioning that complaint phone calls have come in from three clients this month, you might say, "Three complaint calls in a month are unacceptable because the customers are sure to go elsewhere."

Third, *stay focused on solutions.* Make it clear that the purpose of the communication is to move things forward: "We need both to win back their confidence and to show them you are responsive. For example, you could do a free analysis of their systems."

■ Challenges to Respectful Engagement

The yield from respectful engagement is clear in terms of building a pathway to high-quality connection. Despite the attraction of respectful engagement for both parties and the full menu of possible strategies available for cultivating it, most people at work say they don't get enough of this kind of interaction. Why would this be the case? I believe it is because everyone has to contend with several important challenges to respectful engagement. Here I will identify three specific challenges, but there are inevitably many more. None of the challenges I discuss have simple fixes. Some of the challenges are minimized by being in an organization that fosters the building of high-quality connections, which is the focus of Chapter Six. More generally, it's important to realize that everyone will be better and worse at various times in being able to successfully overcome challenges to any of the strategies for connection building discussed in this book. Like any competence, building high-quality connections takes practice. It often requires a change of mindset.

Challenge #1: Depleted Resources

It's a well-known fact: these days organizations want more from their employees for less. Put this fact up against people's limited physical, emotional, and intellectual resources, and the work of respectful engagement starts to look tough. When people are spent because of the time and resources they invest in the simple requirements of their work, often being respectful is seen as an additional burden, requiring an expenditure of energy that people simply don't have.

This challenge is not easy to answer. Here are three measures to consider:

- *Keep reminding yourself of the value of this important activity.* Hold in your mind a vivid example of when someone engaged you respectfully and remember the difference it made.
- *Start small.* Pick a particular meeting or occasion in which you will consciously work to apply one of the important elements of respectful engagement. For example, try turning off your computer or unplugging your phone when someone enters the room to talk with you.
- *Be attentive to what happens when you repeatedly engage others respectfully.* Notice the payoffs, and see whether they aren't saving you time and energy in the long run.

Challenge #2: Power Matters

Where people sit in the organization affects what they pay attention to. The disconcerting news from psychology is that people in higher-status roles pay less attention to those who are below them than lower-status people pay to higher-status ones.[32] Even worse, they rarely recognize it. As a result, if you are trying to build connection across levels in an organization and you are in a lower power position, you have a tougher row to hoe than those who are power-endowed. Respectful engagement, which is based on people being present and attending to each other, is more challenging when you are trying to build connection across levels. Here are suggestions for minimizing power effects:

- *Be aware of the problem.* If you have power over someone else and think you are conveying attention, know you may have blinders on. Seek feedback. Ask people working for you if they experience you as being present, affirming them, listening effectively, and communicating in a supportive way.
- *Take steps to minimize power and status differences.* If you are the person with more power, consider small moves that reduce this advantage. Try meeting where you are on even ground, for example, in a conference room instead of your office. Do not emphasize status differences through the use of formal titles or other formal authority signals.

Challenge #3: Virtual Respectful Engagement?

Respectful engagement is easier to do in face-to-face encounters than it is in virtual connections such as e-mail. Respectful engagement relies on subtle cues of body, gesture, and voice that are difficult to convey electronically. Consider these strategies:

- *Take measures to communicate in person on a regular basis.* Treat seriously the need to make extra efforts to create and maintain respect in person to offset the challenge of creating this form of connection in virtual communications.
- *Augment e-mail with communication by phone.* Consider using additional visual means such as small video camera images available through technology that display a richer set of visual cues for communication.

■ Putting Respectful Engagement to Work

No change will happen in your own effectiveness at building high-quality connections unless you pause to reflect, assess, and actually try new ways of interrelating. Changing the manner of connection to others is often harder than other kinds of changes because the associated habits are so deeply ingrained. At the same time, the yield from such changes can be quite extraordinary for you and for your work organization.

Assessment

Now is the time to make these more abstract ideas of respectful engagement real in your work life. This section asks you to do a quick assessment of the degree to which you are using respectful engagement to build and sustain relationships at work. This assessment has three goals: to increase awareness of the connecting methods you are currently using and not using, to reflect on which methods are and are not working, and to experiment with new ways of connecting that will increase the chances of building high-quality connections.

In doing these assessments and the reflections that follow, I recommend that you acquire some form of journal or dedicated space for reflecting, recording, and building on the important insights. You will be amazed at the wealth of knowledge you acquire based on the wellspring of your own experience. The assessment and reflective exercises are set up on the assumption that you are using some form of connecting journal.

Step 1
Recall a specific interaction that you have had with a peer, boss, subordinate, or customer during the last two days. It's important to take a moment and visualize the interaction in detail.

Step 2
In the columns allotted in Exhibit 2.1, jot down the degree to which you and the other person used the various means that are part of respectful engagement in how you interacted with each other.

Exhibit 2.1. **Assessing Respectful Engagement**

Jot down details of a specific interaction:

_____

_____

_____

To what extent did each of you use these means of respectful engagement?	Myself	Other
▪ Conveying presence		
▪ Being genuine		
▪ Communicating affirmation		
▪ Effective listening		
▪ Supportive communication		
Outcomes of the interaction for you and for the other person:		
▪ More energy?		
▪ Positive regard?		
▪ Felt mutuality?		
▪ Other?		

Step 3

Consider the outcomes of the interaction. How did it leave you feeling? How did it leave your interaction partner feeling? In your outcome assessment be sure to consider at least three indicators of being in a high-quality connection:

- Did you experience an energy charge? Did you feel a heightened sense of vitality and energy for action?
- Did you experience a sense of positive regard or resonance— a momentary but powerful sense of acceptance from the other person?
- Did you experience a sense of mutuality, meaning a sense of engagement and participation in the interaction?

Step 4

Ask yourself how typical this type of pattern of respectful engagement is in your work interactions, and why.

Next Steps: Further Reflection and Action Stretches

This type of assessment is only useful to the degree that it generates insight and gives you a basis for affirming or altering your future connecting behavior. Remember the ultimate goal of these reflections and actions is to increase the quality of connections you build and sustain at work. Here are four further reflections followed by several recommended actions, all designed to help make this goal a reality.

Reflection

Which aspects of respectful engagement seem easiest for you? Which are the most challenging?

Action. Make a commitment to try out an underutilized means of respectful engagement this week in a relationship that you wish to energize.

Action. Seek feedback about whether the tactics you are using, the ones that seem easiest, are in fact working.

Reflection
Are you using the full spectrum of means of respectful engagement? If not, here are some specific actions to try:

Action. Practice presence. Try to listen to someone tomorrow at work with stillness. Don't interrupt. Consciously remove any physical or emotional barriers to making a genuine connection.

Action. Practice affirmation by using everyday occasions (meeting introductions, chance encounters in the hall) to express what you value in other individuals. Do not assume that they know.

Action. Practice genuineness by sharing one true experience about yourself that you have not shared before.

Action. Practice effective listening by being more active through inquiry and clarification questions. Try giving what you heard in your own words to see whether you listened correctly.

Action. Try using the specific techniques of supportive communication (make requests, not demands; be specific; be descriptive rather than evaluative).

Reflection
Note in what circumstances (people, projects, and settings) you are most comfortable respectfully engaging others. Tune in to why these circumstances are most conducive to this form of connection.

Action. Try to increase the favorability of circumstances for respectfully engaging others. Actively seek out situations (projects, people) where you are motivated to respectfully engage.

Reflection

Note in what circumstances (people, project, and settings) those you work with most often respectfully engage you. Ask yourself, why is this happening in these conditions? Is there something about the setting, the timing, the project that is making it easier for people to respectfully engage you? Reflect on this and then actively navigate to be available in settings and at times when people can respectfully engage you.

CHAPTER SUMMARY

The first pathway to building high-quality connections is respectful engagement, which means interacting with someone so that you convey a sense of the person's worth and value. The five strategies for respectful engagement described here are being present, conveying affirmation, being genuine, active listening, and supportive communication.

You can practice being present by minimizing distraction, using present body language, and being available. Communicating affirmation can be achieved by looking for the value in another person, communicating recognition, expressing genuine interest, and treating time as precious. Effective listening involves both empathy and active listening. Finally, supportive communication can be achieved through reliance on requests as opposed to demands, communicating in specific rather than general terms, and making statements descriptive rather than evaluative.

You may face several challenges as you put respectful engagement into practice, including limited resources, power differences, and more virtual than real communication opportunities. Overcoming these challenges involves reinforcing your belief in the power of this connecting method through vivid reminders from your own experience, making active attempts to minimize power differences, and augmenting virtual communication with real face-to-face chances to connect.

You can put respectful engagement to work by assessing your current patterns of interaction and committing to trying one or more of these strategies presented in this chapter, beginning today.

Task Enabling

M y physician tells two very different tales about being an internist in group practices. In practice one, the physicians were highly trained and experienced specialists with extraordinarily busy schedules, a well-oiled staff office, a solid reputation, and a large waiting list of patients wishing to be seen. However, the doctors talked to one another only sporadically. When they did, it was rarely to share new ideas or attempt to resolve vexing diagnoses. The doctors did not accommodate each other in any way. They worked as separate professionals. My doctor left the practice after just two years because she felt only loosely connected to the group and to the other physicians.

Worse, she did not feel she was learning at the same rate as colleagues in other practices.

When she joined Michigan Healthcare, the difference in the connection between people was palpable. The office felt warm, energetic, and alive. Doctors helped each other out by sharing resources such as current medical articles they knew would be of interest to their colleagues. They helped each other figure out tough diagnoses. They saw each other's patients if their experience equipped them better to understand and treat a patient's symptoms and underlying illness. The doctors in the practice also routinely covered for each other when there were family emergencies. As my doctor described it, the whole feel of the place was different from her previous practice. Michigan Healthcare had such a great reputation that it had long waiting lists not only of patients but of doctors eager to join the practice. And it wasn't just that the office was an unusually pleasant place to work. My doctor speaks glowingly about how the interactions with her colleagues have contributed to her professional growth by broadening her experience and expertise.

What makes these two organizational contexts so different? A major part of the answer is the level of *task enabling* going on among the professionals who worked in each practice. Task enabling comprises the various strategies people use to facilitate the successful performance of others. In the case of my doctor's experience, doctors task enabled each other when they shared resources, jointly thought through tough cases, or rearranged their schedules to accommodate their colleagues' and patients' needs.

Task enabling resembles what one successful basketball coach, Phil Jackson, calls "invisible leadership." Jackson, former longtime coach of the Chicago Bulls, describes his coaching style as a middle path between control and laissez-faire. It has at its heart principles of task enabling. Jackson creates a supportive environment that structures the way team members relate to each other, giving them the freedom to realize their potential.[1] Like a good musical accompanist or a magnificent teacher, the task enabler plays a supporting role that becomes visible in the enhanced performance of others.

As with the other pathways to building high-quality connections, task enabling generates energy and commitment. Johann Driber, a managerial consultant who had recently moved to a different unit with another boss, reflected on the difference task enabling made in the unit's performance and in his own motivation to perform well:

> During a job interview I talked at length with several people who worked in the same type of position. What they told me about the boss was really encouraging. They said that one of his highest priorities was to remove obstacles from the paths of the employees so that they could serve customers in better ways. They also said that he had created a strong spirit of teamwork among everyone in the department. I had come from an environment where the boss gave lots of detailed orders, and it was hard to believe that this work setting could be so different. He was actually there to help people do their jobs better. After I took the job I found that my coworkers' comments were, if anything, understated. People enjoyed their work, they helped each other when deadlines were approaching, and they had the strongest commitment to improving the department's outcomes of any workplace I have ever experienced. I've never worked so hard and yet so enjoyed a job, and the people I worked with, in my entire career.

Task enabling is the second very important pathway by which people build high-quality connections with each other at work. Although it resembles a style of leadership—in fact, it can be an important component of leadership—it can happen between people at all levels in the organization. Bosses can enable subordinates. Subordinates can enable their superiors. Peers can enable peers. As in the case of my doctor's experience at Michigan Healthcare, the effects on both individuals and the organization can be profound and lasting.

■ The Power of Task Enabling

In work organizations, task-enabling strategies improve others' performance at the same time that they help build high-quality connections. Task enabling builds more vibrant connections in three main ways. First, when one person at work enables another, an investment of resources flows from one to the other. These investments come in many forms: time, advice, experience, motivation, organization, money, and so on. Investing in others in this way makes them better off, building their desire to invest in return. This reciprocal investment process makes the connection stronger and more vibrant. Matt Downs, a software engineer known for his dedication to helping others with technical problems, articulates the sentiment about helping another person learn that often underlies task enabling: "I want to facilitate the learning process. I want them to learn to do it by themselves. When I help, I try to do enough to enable them to learn to do it on their own. I push them away to make them try. . . . I welcome them back if they need more direction."[2]

Similarly, at Southwest Airlines supervisors explicitly think of their role as one of serving their direct reports and facilitating their learning: "We are here to help them do their jobs."[3] In both examples the attitude and actions of task enabling create a positive cycle of feedback and growth that enhances performance and builds connection.

The second way task enabling builds connection is by communicating positive regard and affirmation to another person.

Simple acts of helping that make another person's job easier communicate an awareness of and valuing of someone else's work. As I discussed in Chapter Two, this type of respectful engagement is a powerful means for creating high-quality connections. As with respectful engagement, small task-enabling actions can be very powerful. When a coworker anticipates your need to be debriefed about an important issue that may affect your work project, this act of enabling simultaneously helps you perform better and sends a signal of mutual regard. I am always amazed at how my secretary enables me in almost every domain of my work life by anticipating and correcting errors, informing me of things on the horizon that I am not thinking about, or making simple gestures like ensuring that the kinds of folders and pens I like are readily available in the supply cabinet.

The third way task enabling builds connection is by transforming the task enabler's self-image. Those who enable the successful performance of others experience a heightened sense of personal worth. Ram Dass and Paul Gorman, writers who have explored the art of helping in all walks of life, describe the transformation this way, "You yourself feel transformed and connected to a deeper sense of identity."[4] That enhanced sense of worth and identity leads to further efforts to build connection. Psychologists have found that the positive emotion of pride provides an intrinsic reward for people who help others. This experience of pride, in turn, helps them to imagine a future in which they do more significant helping. And so another virtuous cycle forms: task enabling builds more desire to enable, and each enabling act deepens connections with others.

As this last point suggests, investing in others is an investment in oneself. The process at work is mutually empowering at the same time that it is building connection. An engineer describes the value she gets from helping colleagues learn difficult calculations essential to their performance:

Yeah, actually it sets [strengthens] my knowledge too . . . because I have to explain it. And I like teaching, and I like showing people something new and a new way to look at things and try to put it in their terms and such. And I get a lot out of it because I really cement my knowledge, if I can explain, like a variance. If I can explain the variance calculation to somebody in a way that they can understand it, then I understand it much better. And I've learned a lot more doing than I learned at school taking tests and following the applied methodology.[5]

When acts of enabling are multiplied through an organization and the quality of connections between people is strengthened, the organization's capacity to learn and adapt improves. Organizational learning requires that people be able to take risks, experiment with new ways of doing things, and make mistakes. You can easily see how being in a place where people working beside, below, and above you enable one another creates a much safer environment for trying out new things. At the same time, where enabling happens easily and freely, people move up the learning curve much more quickly in figuring out how to make things work effectively. Finally, where a lot of enabling is happening, mistakes are more quickly detected and corrected.

■ How to Create Task Enabling

Task enabling offers a rich menu of possibilities for building connection. In this section I highlight a number of specific behaviors, grouped under five general strategies:

- *Teaching* focuses on providing information that allows people to do tasks more effectively.

- *Designing* focuses on enabling others by selecting and arranging features of the job to make it more interesting and appealing to the job holder.
- *Advocating* focuses on helping others perform by easing the navigation of the political context of the organization.
- *Accommodating* focuses altering the substance, timing, or process of what you are doing to enable others to succeed with their work.
- *Nurturing* focuses on individuals' developmental needs in a way that helps them perform more effectively.[6]

For any of these actions to work, they must be done with the mindset of mutuality. This means that the actions must be engaged with openness to the feelings and thoughts of the other person at the same time that one is open to having one's own feelings and actions changed by those of the other.[7] As with all the other skills that build high-quality connections, the *way* you approach task enabling will have a major effect on whether your actions generate high-quality connections with others.

Teaching

Teaching is a critical form of task enabling that can be done formally or informally, in big forums or around the water cooler. Task enabling through teaching happens whenever one person offers information, guidance, or a morsel of advice that enables others to conduct their work more easily.

Sometimes teaching means helping an individual understand different situations and offering new ways to think about approaching tasks. One of my business school colleagues, Jim Hines, enabled me this way recently. In an offhanded way I had mentioned being stuck and stalled on a chapter while writing this book. Jim offered a story that he had found instructive for overcoming his own writing blocks. The story was of a famous biologist who set aside the same two hours a day to write and followed a ritualistic routine for "getting in the mood" before he began his two-hour stint. The routine involved the way he positioned his chair, the pen he used to write, and the lamp that lit the pages. Jim may not have thought of what he was doing as teaching, but the story was just what I needed to help me see another way of approaching the writing task. The task enabling affirmed the value of our colleagueship, and the quality of our connection was taken up a notch.

Of course, teaching is often done quite deliberately. Three distinct forms of teaching that are particularly relevant in organizations are training, coaching, and political assisting.

Seen as task enabling, training involves providing others with opportunities to learn material that helps them perform their work more effectively. Training often involves strengthening specific job-related skills, but equally important is the broader type of training that builds basic knowledge relevant to excellent performance.

We all know that training is particularly important when people are getting started on new tasks or in a new organization. These junctures provide critical opportunities for building vibrant connections between people and between people and the firm. When MBA students in my classes describe the poor job most firms do in training their interns, it reminds me that we cannot take task enabling for granted. In their case, and in the case of most people in organizations, when opportunities for training are present and not delivered on, not only is a chance to form a meaningful connection forgone but employees withdraw commitment and engagement for the organization. Poor task enabling can undercut employee loyalty and attachment.

By the same token, effective training can powerfully enable others. Just ask Jon Orto, a new technical consultant hired by Netsolve, about the difference it made to have Craig Tysdal—the company's president and CEO—teaching the three-day module on customer service to all the new employees from secretaries on up. Craig Tysdal was enabling everyone who attended this event by teaching the value of customer service and its centrality to the company, but also by the small tidbits and stories that he shared about what really works in customer service at Netsolve.[8]

The second form of teaching, coaching, involves sharing specific strategies for accomplishing career goals. Coaching is one of the reasons mentoring programs have been so critical to individuals' career success. Mentoring programs are often explicitly designed to routinize the coaching activities between more seasoned and less seasoned members of the organization. These programs often help people succeed in terms of greater higher career outcomes and satisfaction, and they also create task-enabling opportunities that build higher-quality connections between mentors and those they work with.[9]

The third form of teaching, political assisting, happens when one person provides another with information about organizational or professional politics. Everyone knows that organizations are inherently, sometimes intensely, political. Patterns of action and resource allocation are tied to the self-interests of organizational members as well to organizational interests. Sometimes the motives and dynamics underlying politically motivated behaviors are difficult to discern. When people share knowledge about tactics of influence that work in a unit or warn a colleague or subordinate about political landmines, they are task enabling through political assisting.

All these forms of teaching can be done in a more or less empathetic way. Joyce Fletcher has studied the daily activities of engineers by shadowing them—that is, following them around—during their work day, tracking the types of conversations they have, and then talking with the engineers about what was going on in the conversations. She singles out what she calls "empathetic teaching" as an important form of task enabling.

Empathetic teaching differs from more traditional images of teaching in that it actively considers the other person's readiness to hear and factors in how to say things in way that takes the other person's concerns, fears, and doubts into account. Empathy is the lubricant that smooths the connection forged through teaching. As one engineer put it: "Statistics is an expertise that people are interested in and they want to know it, but they are getting negative feedback from their managers when it takes them a long time to do an analysis or to design an experiment. So, they have a lot of discouragement to learning. So, if you turn them off at all, you've lost them. So in that case I always teach things so I try not to bruise an ego."[10]

Another challenge in teaching is to neutralize the status difference between the teacher and the person being taught. The engineers that Fletcher studied taught her about the power of using collaborative language and communicating an equality of status by means of body language in order to create a feeling of mutuality rather than dominance. For example, to minimize experienced status differences engineers would physically sit down with someone, to be at their level, rather than stand up and tower over them when they were trying to teach a new skill or program. This sense of mutuality makes enabling through teaching more effective for building high-quality connections. It also breeds cooperation between people, helping the firm accomplish more collaborative work.

Designing

There's plenty of evidence that changing the way jobs are designed increases how motivating people find them, contributing positively to job success. In thinking about job design from a task-enabling point of view, it's useful to focus on how to help others succeed at a job by encouraging them to rearrange or alter its component parts. Although the real possibility set is much greater, this section singles out six ways to do this form of task enabling:

- Task chunking
- Enhanced variety
- Task reallocation
- Increased autonomy
- Clear significance
- Process facilitation

Chunking

Sometimes the tasks that compose a job are overwhelming in scope or scale, deflating anyone's sense that they can succeed. In these cases, helping another through task chunking can be an effective enabling and connecting strategy. *Task chunking* involves breaking a task up into doable parts. This tactic resonates with the idea of small wins.[11] Parsing big jobs into smaller bits helps people see them as more feasible to do and builds momentum through the small wins of seeing the smaller bits completed.

Variety

At the opposite end of the spectrum are jobs that people find too simple, boring, or monotonous. In such cases, an appropriate enabling tactic is adding variety to make the job more interesting and motivating. Research has shown that increasing task variety can elevate a person's job satisfaction and performance.[12] You can increase task variety by adding a wider range of tasks to a job (that is, by job enlargement and job enrichment) or by rotating people through different job assignments. In either case, people's engagement in the job increases because they can put a broader array of their talents and skills to use.

Reallocation

A third approach to enabling through job design involves reallocating tasks so that people can focus on those tasks they do well and that bring them the greatest job satisfaction. For example, suppose two employees are doing the same type of work yet they each like and excel at different parts of their jobs. It may be possible for them to trade aspects of their jobs so that they can each focus more on the kind of work that brings them the greatest satisfaction.

Autonomy

A fourth enabling strategy is to enhance the level of autonomy that people have to do their work. Designers of empowerment and participation programs know that increasing people's control over the means of doing their work enhances motivation. More generally, it enables people's performance to increase the control they have over the means and timing of doing their work. Beth, an administrator in a university setting, describes the difference it made to be granted autonomy by her faculty boss and how it made her feel: "It pretty much turned out that he actually let me run the whole thing. . . . I would just keep him informed of what was going on. . . . [I would say to him,] 'I've got this assembled, do you want to see it before I send it over,' and he actually said, 'No that's okay.' I mean, he didn't even check it because he felt confident enough that I had done it for so long. . . . So that was a really good experience."

It is easy to hear in Beth's words the power of this form of task enabling to strengthen the quality of her connection with her boss as well as her sense of motivation and job satisfaction.

Significance

A fifth strategy is helping to frame the significance of the job in a meaningful and compelling way. Leaders can enable a whole firm by framing the significance of the organization's activities.

For example, Max DePree, former CEO of Herman Miller, re-framed the significance of the company's work of making furniture when he declared that making furniture the Herman Miller way was "a gift to the human spirit."[13] At a more mundane, day-to-day level, anyone can enable others by helping them see the value in what they are doing. In research that my colleagues and I have done on the work of hospital cleaners, several participants told us about the effects of being trained by other cleaners who saw the cleaning function as central to the mission of providing effective healing to the patients.

Process
A final form of task enabling is process facilitation, whereby one individual helps a collective by observing and helping to improve the effectiveness of its processes. For example, facilitation could involve making sure that members of the group are interacting in ways that are consistent with achieving the group or team's desired outcomes. Susan Ping, longtime facilitator of teams, calls this form of enabling "working the magic," meaning unlocking positive communication and interaction patterns so a group's process contributes to its effectiveness.

Advocating

In discussing teaching, I mentioned political assisting as a way to help others function effectively in an organization. Advocating is a more active task-enabling strategy for facilitating people's success in the political arena of the organization. All organizations have a shadow structure (outside of the official organizational hierarchy) that determines who has and who does not have power.[14] Most organizations are fraught with political landmines and barriers. Advocates help others navigate the political landscape by opening access to the right people, places, and resources.

One important form of advocating involves providing exposure and visibility for another person. Accompanying people to important company events, arranging meetings with the right people at the right times, and creating opportunities for people to demonstrate their abilities are all concrete actions that provide exposure and visibility.

This form of advocacy can involve acting as a matchmaker by connecting a subordinate, a peer, or even a boss to other individuals who are important to their job performance and success. Facilitating connections helps shape another person's network, thus improving the individual's access to jobs, information, power, and reputation.[15]

A striking example comes from a university context, where freshly minted Ph.D.'s, like junior employees in most companies, are highly dependent on more senior people to provide them with exposure opportunities. One senior faculty member reflected on a bold enabling move made by his former thesis chairman and the difference it made for access to publication outlets and jobs:

> I took the first job at Middle State, and it was my first year there. I was invited back to [my graduate school] to give a talk . . . and my chairman had also invited Mr. Important, the Nobel laureate, to a workshop. He managed to have us go back on the same plane flight. He orchestrated the whole thing, and during [the flight], I had this Nobel laureate to myself—and the next thing I know. . . . I had a call from Prestige University to see if I was interested in a permanent job. . . . This all evolved out of that orchestrated encounter. . . . Just the idea that they were interested was amazing at that stage, [given my] coming from a sort of no name sort of place. . . . I think that relationship and contacts made it even easier to publish in Prestige U's journal as well.[16]

Advocating can also take the form of championing, or actively promoting, someone's abilities, potential, and competence.

Championing is a more public and proactive tactic than simply providing exposure and visibility. It is most effective if the champion is credible and legitimate, able to boost the power of the person who is being sponsored through power-by-association effects.[17]

Conflicts and controversies can derail people from organizational success tracks. A useful but more defensive means for enabling others in the political scene involves protecting. *Protecting* refers to shielding others from tough situations that would put them at risk. Often this form of advocating is done by senior managers for more junior colleagues who are less experienced or knowledgeable about a situation and thus may inadvertently get in organizational harm's way. A participant in management expert Kathy Kram's study of mentoring described his protecting actions this way:

> I tried to protect him from the outside world until I felt he was ready to be seen. I had spent an awful lot of time in that area and when I sent him back, I knew he knew the environment— the likes and dislikes of my superiors and the general inner workings of the department; the inner relationships of various people, too, who could be trusted and who couldn't be trusted and stuff like that. So I pretty much kept Dick under wraps in terms of other people seeing him for several months, until I, from my own relationship with him, I could judge that he had picked up enough knowledge and could handle himself well enough.[18]

A final form of advocating involves providing material support to help another person perform a job. Having the material supplies needed to do one's job is by no means guaranteed. Managers, especially, can have a major impact on others' success (and build higher-quality connections along the way) by providing access to essential resources. These resources may be basics such as office space, supplies, and secretarial support, or they may be more discretionary matters such as technical support or advanced training that are difficult for individuals to access on their own.

Accommodating

The strategy of accommodating involves adjusting the timing, intensity, or scope of your own activity to allow others to succeed at their tasks—that is, changing the schedule, pace, or sequence in which you accomplish tasks so that subordinates can better get their work done. This form of enabling makes interdependence at work very transparent. By adjusting your own work or expectations to grant another person time or discretion, you release the power of that interdependence and invest it in building connection.

Sometimes accommodating involves cutting other people some slack to help them succeed with their job. For example, extending deadlines or reducing required time at the office when their performance suffers because they are going through an emotional situation or some other form of stress is one important way of enabling by accommodating.[19] Small acts of accommodating individuals' life circumstances to enable them to do their work affirm them as whole people as opposed to just work-centered employees.

I have been studying people's experience of compassion at work and the difference it makes for them as employees and for the firm as a whole. Over and over again employees have told our research team about the powerful impact of others' actions that grant them flexibility to do their work on their own terms given the pain or trauma they are dealing with. For example, when my friend John Crene's mother was dying after a long bout with cancer, his colleagues (all partners in his law firm) took on extra work and covered for him at meetings so he had more flexibility in his schedule over the last few weeks of her illness. The improvised change in arrangements around meetings and work time granted John the flexibility to take care of important personal matters without sacrificing work performance. As a result, he experienced not only gratitude but a sense of being affirmed. These feelings paved the way for a higher-quality connection to the people who made this possible, and strengthened his loyalty to the firm.

A second and more active form of accommodating involves adjusting the execution of tasks to facilitate another person's work. For example, peers at work can accommodate each other's fluctuating workloads to help one another succeed. Brenda Diego, a senior staff coordinator in a busy university unit, talked about how she valued other people's willingness to enable her by taking on additional tasks when she was overloaded: "We were all involved in bringing these speakers here and making all of the arrangements that were expected. . . . Most of the work had to be done in the last week or two . . . I had so much to do that was directly related to my work . . . I felt very positive working with these other [people]. . . . They were all very willing and understanding, . . . [if I said] 'I'm really tied down right now. Could one or the other of you possibly handle this task?' So that was I'd say very positive."[20]

As a manager, you can actively encourage a spirit of accommodation among employees. For example, you can encourage joint problem-solving and creative thinking on the part of the group when individuals need some form of accommodation. In some circumstances, a good technique is to create partnerships where two or more people share responsibility for a joint project and are encouraged to accommodate each other. Perhaps most important, you can model accommodating behavior yourself by the way you adjust your own work and pitch in to facilitate others' success.

Nurturing

Nurturing strategies involve helping others succeed at work by addressing their developmental needs, that is, issues of personal growth, identity, and competence. I call this form of task enabling *nurturing* because it focuses on providing emotional support and taking actions that help people develop and grow. This kind of task enabling is often more personal and psychologically deeper than the other enabling strategies.

One common form of nurturing is role modeling. At the heart of role modeling is a type of identification process whereby one person consciously or unconsciously wishes to take on pieces of the identity of the other person.[21] As role model, you take advantage of the fact that another person is trying to emulate you by setting an example of what it means to be successful in a certain role. Indirectly, your acceptance of this emotional identification with you facilitates the other person's success. Here is a subordinate describing the effects of role modeling his boss, Michael: "I came to work for Michael about a year and a half ago. He is just a super guy. I've never met anybody like him before in the company. . . . I think what he does most for me—is just by his example. He's a model that you watch and see how he works. He is just an interesting guy. I'm learning a higher order of organizational skills that I will take with me where I go."[22]

You can also enable others through nurturing more directly by providing personal counseling. This enabling tactic differs from coaching in that it involves providing support and advice about personal concerns that may not be immediately or directly related to someone's job or career. By being available to others in this way, you can create a secure base that allows them to be more authentically themselves and to display vulnerability about issues of concern.[23] This is yet another way of affirming others in their whole being, not just in their narrow role as workers. It is worth mentioning that sometimes personal counseling may involve active listening—simply being present and actively hearing what another person's live concerns are. In this case, no further assistance is needed beyond availability. However, other times, personal counseling may require advising someone on issues you do not feel comfortable or trained to handle. In such cases, effective enabling can involve helping that person gain access to professional help or advice that is suited to the issue at hand.

Often personal counseling concerns issues of values or life demands and takes the form of sharing your own experience in a way that makes it useful to others, perhaps by helping them avoid missteps you have made. One senior manager described the way he provided counsel to Dick, a younger manager in his firm: "I was the same totally committed work type person for a number of years as Dick was. And I saw him going the same road where I had been. When I developed more perspective myself, I changed and I guess I was trying to explain to him that he probably will change too, and why doesn't he start thinking now about it—he might gain three or four years that I lost."[24]

Nurturing can also take the form of motivating someone through encouragement. Everyone knows firsthand that encouragement is a valuable emotional reward that helps bring more energy to bear on a task. Here's an example of the transforming effect of a manager's use of encouragement and praise on both the manager and the people she was working with. In this case, Nicola is the general manager of a financial services company. The two management experts Kouzes and Posner describe how Nicola's nurturing of her employees by encouraging them changed her own felt connection to the group: "Nicola felt vulnerable opening herself up like that to thank the group. But she knew for sure that she'd established a human connection with her colleagues that hadn't been there before and would be highly beneficial in the months ahead. . . . In the following weeks she brought much more of herself to her work relationships, and people responded with a new level of enthusiasm for her leadership. . . . She felt more energetic than ever as she came to work, and when she went home she felt an increasing satisfaction in what she'd accomplished."[25]

Like the other enabling strategies, nurturing in all its forms makes demands on those who apply it. First, it requires you to be attentive to others' needs and alert to opportunities to help them grow. Second, it requires you to give something of yourself to invest actively in others' success. As others feel that investment, your connection with them is strengthened and deepened.

■ Challenges in Task Enabling

A number of challenges stand in the way of effective task enabling. Being aware of the challenges is helpful, but even more useful are suggestions for how to overcome the challenges. I offer a start at both in this section.

Challenge #1: The Difficulties of Timing

Task enabling works best when its timing allows the person who is being enabled to fully use the help or assistance. While that sounds easy, effectively timed task enabling is a challenge. Often people want or need help at a moment when others are not prepared to give it. Similarly, with the best of intentions people sometimes give or offer help when others are not prepared to receive it. In either case, a task-enabling opportunity is wasted and a chance for building higher-quality connection is lost. Here is a process that can help you deal with this challenge:

- *Begin by communicating a desire to do task enabling.* Just making this goal explicit will motivate peers, subordinates, and even bosses to set aside time to talk about this important subject.

- *Arrange for a regular specific occasion in which to have conversations about task enabling.* Make sure to give your colleague time to prepare for the meeting. Talk about ways you have enabled each other successfully in the past and what kind of enabling you wish to do for each other in the future. Decide together on specific steps to take.
- *Every six months seek feedback regarding how the enabling is working.*

This three-step process will not only ensure that you and your partner make time to discern what enabling each of you need, it will also improve the rate at which you learn to enable each other.

Challenge #2: Barriers to Seeking Help

Enabling is often easier and more effective if it's clear that someone wants help. But seeking help in many organizations is a rare event. A number of factors stop people from going out on a limb and asking for help at work, even when they desperately need it.[26] For example, people may worry about the impression they create when they ask for help. They may feel that asking for help undermines their own sense of competence. Or they may resist seeking help because they do not want to feel dependent on others.

The way to counter such worries is to discern when help is needed or would be useful and initiate the process rather than waiting to be asked. More generally, as a manager you can help cultivate a climate in which help seeking is seen as not only normal but desirable, as Hollie describes in this statement about her manager, Marie: "Something else that she's taught me is that it's OK to say that I need help. There was one instance where I needed help in doing something, I tried to do it myself once or twice and it didn't work out. She pushed me to come to her and let me know I could make a mistake and she would still support me."[27]

Here are specific suggestions for overcoming people's resistance to seeking help:

- *Assume that people you are working with experience hesitancy about seeking help.* Emphasize the importance of seeking help to grow, to learn, and to improve. Make sure that people understand that seeking help is normal, expected, and desirable behavior.
- *Reward help seeking when it happens.* Verbal affirmations will reinforce the inclination to ask for help. In addition, set things up to make it likely that people will get help when they seek it, so the full loop of task enabling can be experienced.

Challenge #3: Devaluing of Task Enabling

The third challenge in task enabling is probably the most difficult to overcome because it reflects values that are firmly woven into Western culture. The high value our culture assigns to self-reliance, independence, and individual achievement works against the recognition and rewarding of task enabling. Often task enabling and other forms of helping are not seen as the real work of the organization and thus not the appropriate and valued work of competent employees; indeed, some have argued that in many organizations task enabling is seen as weakness and inadequacy as opposed to strength and competent action.[28] Even the intended beneficiaries of task enabling may see it as a weakness. An engineer noted the deliberate efforts she had to make to create antidotes to the devaluing of enabling actions: "If you try to nurture, they just don't get it. They don't understand that is what you are doing. They see it as a weakness, and they use it against you. They don't see that you are doing it consciously. They think you have missed something or that they've gotten something over on you. So, if you try to be nice you end up doing other people's work. I've gotten so that now I say, 'OK, look, I'll help you out on this one. But you owe me one.' "[29]

You may need to work hard at overcoming the deep bias that favors independence over seeking and giving help. Here are two suggestions:

- *Create explicit recognition and rewards for doing task enabling.* Go beyond rewards for mentoring relationships. Allow people to nominate others for the reward who have demonstrated effective enabling.
- *Promote conversation and dialogue about effective task enabling.* Encourage people to share stories about effective task enabling. This kind of sharing can promote appreciation of the range of ways that people can enable others, as well as a recognition of what works.

■ Putting Task Enabling to Work

The first step in putting task enabling to work as a means of building high-quality connections is to assess what you are already doing and what you might change. In this section I offer two assessments. The first assessment will help you get a better handle on who is enabling you, how it is working, and how you might facilitate the ways others are connecting to you. The second looks at the task-enabling strategies you are currently using yourself.

Task-Enabling Map

It's rare for anyone to recognize how much their own performance is facilitated by the often-invisible helping hands of others. This recognition is important for three reasons. First, appreciation of others' task enabling will strengthen your connections to those who assist you. Second, becoming aware of your own need for support is a first step toward improving your own performance by seeking task enabling from others. Third, reflecting on how others enable you will enhance your appreciation of this pathway to connection and inspire you to think of ways you can enable others.

To enhance your appreciation of the task enablers around you, create a task-enabling map.

Step 1: Picture Yourself on Stage

Picture yourself doing a critical performance at work "on stage." For example, you might be developing a new product, managing a project team, or creating a new budget system. The task-enabling map represents the cast of characters who are supporting and helping you with your performance.

Think of your performance as having a front and back stage. The front stage involves work that is visible to others. The back stage is what enables the performance on the front stage, but only you can directly see it or know it is there. It is this back-stage infrastructure that you will map (see Exhibit 3.1).

Step 2: Identify the Enablers

Identify three kinds of backstage enablers who facilitate your performance. *Direct enablers* are visible, easy-to-identify enablers of your performance, people you have regular contact with (support staff, subordinates, bosses). *Sideline enablers* are people who assist you in less direct or obvious but no less critical ways. They may be family members, friends, or people in your organization whose help is not dictated by their job or their formal relationship to you. Finally, *balcony enablers* are the individuals who have inspired you in the past and who have aided you through their inspiration, wisdom, direction, or mere existence. Balcony enablers rarely know that they are playing a role in your current performance.

Step 3: Reward Current Enablers

Ask yourself these two hard questions:

- Do my enablers understand that I recognize the role they are playing in helping me?

Exhibit 3.1. A Task-Enabling Map

Task or project to be mapped: _____

_____

_____

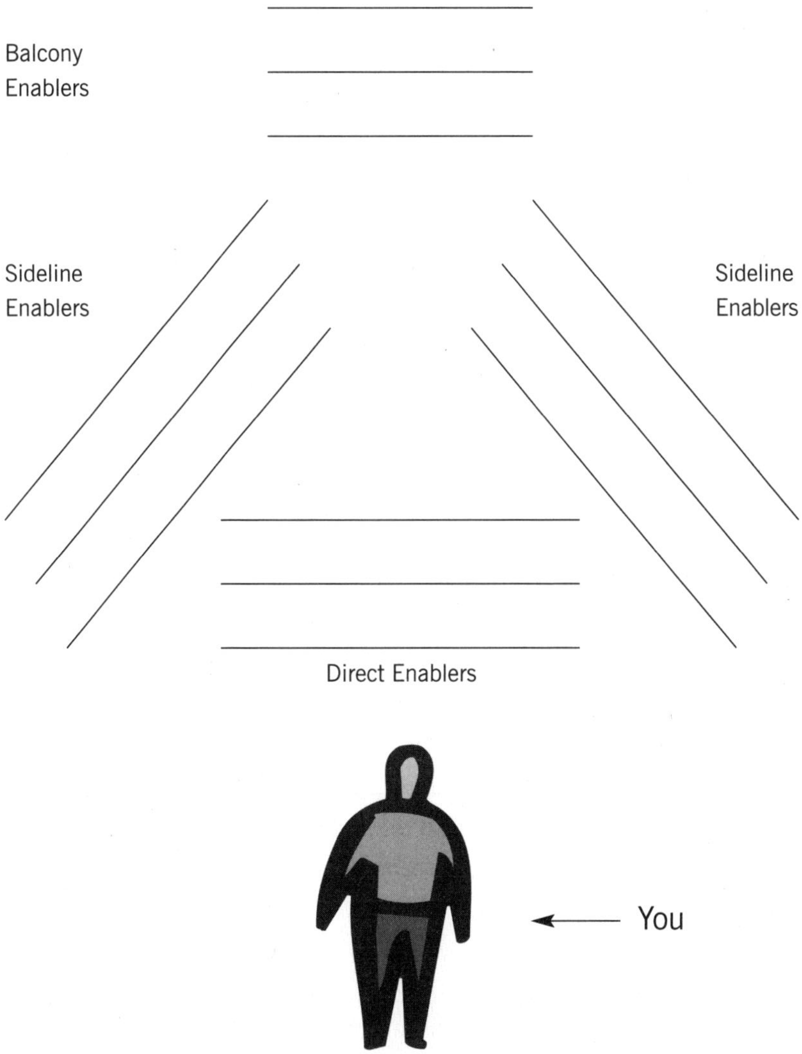

Balcony
Enablers   _____

                            _____

                            _____

Sideline   Sideline
Enablers   Enablers

                    _____

                    _____

                    _____

                    Direct Enablers

←——— You

- Do my enablers know that I appreciate their role in helping me on this project or task?

If you're like most people, the answers are probably no and no. List some concrete things you can do to let your enablers know you recognize and welcome their efforts on your behalf, and some things you can do to reciprocate.

Step 4: Cultivate New Enablers

Your task-enabling map may reveal areas where your current support foundation is weak and you would benefit from new enablers.

- Identify where you currently lack support for this performance.
- Cultivate new enablers by gathering information and recommendations about individuals and groups in your work organization who are effective enablers.
- Remember the importance of mutuality. Consider how you can enable others who are in a position to enable you. Use any of the strategies discussed in this chapter.

Assessing Your Current Strategies

You now should have in mind how others are currently enabling you. It is time to switch perspectives to look at how you are currently enabling others.

Exhibit 3.2 lists the task-enabling strategies that were discussed in this chapter. As I noted at the outset, as a manager you have more forms of enabling are available to you than I list here, but this set of strategies represents a good start for assessing how you are currently using task enabling as a means of building high-quality connections.

Consider each strategy from three perspectives: as a boss (that is, in relation to people who report to you), as a subordinate

Exhibit 3.2. Assessing Your Use of Task Enabling

To what extent do you currently use each means of task enabling?	As a Boss	As a Subordinate	As a Coworker
■ Teaching			
■ Designing			
■ Advocating			
■ Accommodating			
■ Nurturing			
How well is each task-enabling strategy working in each of these roles?			
■ Teaching			
■ Designing			
■ Advocating			
■ Accommodating			
■ Nurturing			
What strategies do you want to use more of in each role?			
■ Teaching			
■ Designing			
■ Advocating			
■ Accommodating			
■ Nurturing			

(in relation to people you report to), and as a coworker (that is, in relation to colleagues at the same level as yourself inside or outside your immediate work group). Assess each strategy in terms of the questions listed.

CHAPTER SUMMARY

Task enabling is a powerful pathway for building connection that engages and energizes individuals while strengthening the learning and adaptation of the work unit or the organization as a whole. This pathway is made up of at least five kinds of actions that create connection by directly or indirectly aiding the performance of a boss, a peer, or a subordinate. *Teaching* involves the sharing of useful knowledge, insight, and information. *Designing* involves structuring features of a job to facilitate another's performance. *Advocating* involves actively helping another navigate the political landscape of the organization. *Accommodating* involves being flexible in ways that enable others to perform better. Finally, *nurturing* involves facilitating others' success by addressing their developmental needs.

All these enabling strategies build connection by creating a dynamic of mutual investment. Those who are enabled feel an enhanced sense of being worthy of investment at the same time that the enablers see themselves as having something worthy to offer. The challenges in task enabling include finding time, overcoming people's resistance to seeking help, and countering the cultural devaluation of task-enabling acts. The chapter offered several suggestions for meeting these challenges, including making deliberate time for task enabling, recognizing and rewarding both help seeking and help giving, and cultivating conversations in which effective strategies for enabling are shared.

Finally, you can improve your capacity to build connections through task enabling by assessing and facilitating how others enable you in your own performances and by recognizing what task enabling strategies you are using effectively in different roles.

4

Trusting

J oe and Zena had been colleagues at IMAP for more than six years, working in the same marketing unit but not on the same project team. They socialized inside and outside of work, in addition to being important sources of ideas and encouragement to each other. All this changed when Zena discovered that Joe had been working on a market plan that directly competed with her group's project. She could understand his need to work on this, especially given the zero-sum and win-at-all-costs mentality that permeated the firm. But she could not understand why Joe never disclosed what he was doing, especially since they had had many conversations about marketing plans on the horizon. Joe's new market plan borrowed many of the ideas that Zena had enthusiastically discussed with him as actions she hoped to implement in her group. She felt betrayed and violated. It would be a long time, if ever, before she could trust him again.

The fracture of trust between Joe and Zena immediately reduced possibilities for collaboration between their marketing teams. News of the violation of trust reduced the teams' willingness to take risks and to share information. The possibility of high performance for an entire unit instantly diminished as distrust between two people led to a deterioration in the quality of information and collaboration between key teams.

It is experiences like Zena and Joe's that teach us not to make our opening move a trusting move. We don't trust because we have been burned in the past. We don't trust because the situation seems not to reward or encourage it. We don't trust because we don't know what a trusting move looks like. We become guarded in our work life and vigilant about protecting ourselves. Trust, we decide is for suckers.

To regain their faith in trust and see its power in building connection, people need stories like Tom Duchene's:

Tom was allocated a group of freshly hired software engineers who were the only available people to staff the high-risk but high-payoff collaborative venture called Signo, a product intended for a newly emerging market in biotechnology. From the opening meeting, their first face-to-face encounter, team members sensed that Tom had a strong belief in their capacity to produce the product on time, even though other teams had tried and failed. Tom had done his homework and knew the histories, talents, and weak sides of each of his team members. He conveyed his confidence in what the team could produce by what he said and what he did not say in the first meeting and throughout the first six months of progress meetings. The team collaborated and set high objectives for the speed of the project's completion and its quality. Tom gave the team members control over how they would monitor their progress and how they would use the meetings to learn from one another and to keep the heat on themselves to make their short-term objectives. Tom fought hard with the bureaucrats at the level above to get access to key material and intellectual resources that the team needed. His actions and his words sent strong signals that he trusted the individuals and the team as a whole to deliver. All this allowed the team to work faster, to learn more quickly from each other, and to take more risks. In short, his trust energized the team, creating a solid platform for high performance.

These two stories illustrate the central role of trust in building connections with others that create energy in the workplace. Acting with trust is not easy. This chapter considers the specific behaviors that create trust, the challenges that can get in the way, and how you can address these challenges in working with others.

■ The Power of Trust

Acting with trust means acting toward others in a way that conveys belief in their *integrity* (consistency between thought and behavior), *dependability* (honesty and reliability) and *benevolence* (desire and willingness to care).[1] In short, trusting involves acting on positive expectations about other people's behavior and intentions. Whether you begin by conveying trust or being trusted, trust takes you in the direction of a higher-quality, life-giving connection to another person.

Trust is a special resource in that it increases with use.[2] If one person acts toward another in a trusting way, the action creates a self-fulfilling cycle.[3] Suppose I act toward you in a trusting way, perhaps by sharing my concerns about how I will perform on a work-related project. You observe the way I am acting, and my act of trust creates expectations that I will act in a trusting way in the future. Because you see me taking a risk by making myself vulnerable to you, you are more willing to reciprocate in kind. First, my first act of trusting toward you calls forth emotional reactions that encourage you to trust me.[4] Second, my act induces you to see me as more reliable and helpful, contributing to your sense of my integrity, benevolence, and dependability in my actions toward you. You see me as trustworthy and this calls forth trust from you. I also see myself acting toward you in a trusting way by sharing sensitive information. So as not to be inconsistent with how I have acted, I start seeing you as more and more trustworthy.

Assuming the exchange is not broken by a breach of trust, this process of mutual trusting will strengthen our belief in each other's trustworthiness. Trust thus creates a higher-quality connection as both people in a trusting connection expect high-integrity behavior from each other. In trusting connections both people experience more freedom to be authentic, to let their guard down, and to be flexible. Less time is spent monitoring or trying to discern intentions of the other person. In a trusting connection, the default value is that you believe the other person is acting with your best interests in mind. Trust feeds learning and flexibility in a unit, as in the opening example of Tom Duchene's team. Despite the short-term challenges of going out on a limb to trust, the long-term value to your own connections and the connections between members of a unit make it well worth the investment.

How to Create Trust

In our wariness about trusting others, we often adopt a "Show me" stance. We say people have to earn our trust, and then sit back and wait for them to do it. When we take the first step in building trust, we become crafters of connecting possibilities. Rather than passively waiting to see whether someone can be trusted, we actively start the virtuous cycle in which trust builds on itself.

We convey trust most clearly when we allow people to see that we are at risk in some way, making our vulnerability and our reliance on others more visible.[5] This is hard to do. Work organizations can be tough contexts for displaying vulnerability. However, it's easy to see the connection between vulnerability, reliance on others, and trust in other domains of life. For example, when we seek medical help we display our vulnerability and dependence on others in ways that make clear that we trust them. We reveal sensitive and precious information. We give up control. We grant others significant responsibility for our fate. These are powerful acts of trust.

We build trust not only by what we say and do but by what we do not say and do. Words and actions can destroy trust at ten times the speed of trust-building.

Trusting By What We Say

Our words send powerful trusting messages. They send signals about our expectations that open or close the door to mutual trust.

By "our words," I don't mean statements to the effect that "I trust you" so much as statements that convey trust implicitly, by the content of what we choose to share with others and the language we use to share it. Both the *what* and the *how* of verbal communication have a major influence on efforts to build trust.

Sharing Valuable Information. Information is a valuable asset in all work organizations. Information is more valuable when it is relevant, rare, and nonsubstitutable. By sharing information that is valuable with others, managers demonstrate that they care and are more reliable. Inevitably managers have valuable information that they can choose to share or not share with their employees. Sharing the information equips people to do their jobs better (as discussed in Chapter Three, on task enabling). It also sends an important signal that the employees are trusted. As New York University professor and expert on trust Dale Zand reminds us, "The flow of accurate, timely information is critical to productive relationships," and it can also help build trust.[6]

In any work-based relationship both parties inevitably have different information. Choosing to share this information can be a first step in building trust. If I share valuable information with you, I send a signal that I trust you will take good care of it, mindful of my vulnerability if the information is misused. For example, in partnering between suppliers and customers, a good relationship often implies being willing to share confidential information. As George Advey, a business manager at Chevron, puts it, the sharing of information has to be sincere and meaningful to build a real partnership (or high-quality connection): "I have observed many companies utilize that phrase that they are 'going to be a partner with our customers,' yet when it comes down to actually living up to the tenets of being a partner, like sharing confidential information such as manufacturing capabilities, future view, capital spending or product development efforts, it often becomes pretty shallow."[7]

In contrast, when real information sharing happens, partnerships and relationships within or across organizational boundaries flourish. Shannon Galvin, the highest-ranking woman in a major hotel chain, successfully negotiated a pay contract with her union employees that involved, for the first time ever, a pay-for-performance component. One important move that contributed to trust building and the constructive settlement involved the sharing of highly confidential financial information with the union. Analysts of her process concluded this about the timing and significance of her information-sharing behaviors: "The way in which Shannon shared the information is also significant. With common financial data at hand, the union and management could agree on what was actually in the pot. Shannon left the spending to the union members. It was money available for their benefits. They knew best how to spend it. If there was a danger in sharing that information, there was an equally potent benefit. It was an act of trust. A signal that they had the makings of a real dialogue."[8]

Self-Disclosure. Disclosing something of ourselves—especially information that makes us vulnerable in some way—is an especially powerful way to convey and generate trust. By its nature, self-disclosure involves risk, which is no doubt one reason why it is often so rare in organizations. Yet many leaders know that appropriate self-disclosure can be a powerful move in the dance of trust in work organizations. Leadership experts James Kouzes and Barry Posner put it this way: "Letting others know what we stand for, what we value, what we want, what we hope for, what we're willing (and not willing) to do means disclosing information about ourselves. That can be risky. . . . But by demonstrating willingness to take such risks, leaders encourage others to reciprocate."[9]

In any conversation with a colleague at work we have the choice of whether or not to be self-revealing. Maureen Burns told me about the first meeting she had with her subordinates after becoming director of research support at the Michigan Business School. During the meeting, she told them that she had always been afraid of every new job and this one was no exception. Her new colleagues looked at her with amazement. None of their former bosses had been so open about their true feelings. Maureen sensed that revealing her fear sent a signal that she trusted her colleagues to use this information appropriately, so that her self-disclosure was a sign of strength rather than a sign of weakness. She believes that they picked up on her signal and interpreted it correctly, and that it spread through their informal networks as a type of trust endowment, paving the way for more trusting relationships.

Hatim Tyabji, former CEO of VeriFone, a very successful high-tech firm bought by Hewlett-Packard in 1997, was known for the sense of trust he conveyed to others. Like Maureen Burns, he displayed his vulnerability in a way that helped to build strong bonds with employees while at the same time contributing to a culture where people could be more open with each other. His managers described a speech that he gave after the merger announcement as indicative of his style and as an example of how he built trust in the wake of this large organizational change. "The employees know when Hatim speaks he's speaking the absolute truth," Katherine Beall observes. "He means it from the heart, and it's often emotional because you know that he's speaking directly to you about what he really feels."[10]

In his speech, Hatim, like Maureen, spoke about his fears. As Lewin and Regine describe it,

> He gave personal anecdotes and among them he talked about sky diving with his sons to illustrate how he dealt with change and fear. "The story is very funny when he tells it," remembers Roger Bertman. "You could see he was scared out of his mind, standing up there with one leg hanging out of the airplane. But you just do it. He conveyed a sense of humanness and vulnerability by saying, 'Hey, you know, I go through this insecurity too.'"[11]

Such revealing of oneself can be transformative of the possibilities in relationships. When we make the first step to be vulnerable, our action can infect the immediate and more distant relationships at work, infusing them with more life. A colleague of Mark Levine, a physician and director of the family practice residence program of Hampt Health in Pennsylvania, shares how he interprets the impact of Mark's being personal and revealing to his staff: "It is not that he didn't care about his people before; it's just that he didn't think to show it. He started talking more personally to staff, asking how their lives were going, and he saw a dramatic shift in the ambience of this workplace and a more collaborative spirit developing."[12]

Using Inclusive Language. The language we use can convey either distance and separateness, or interdependence and trust. The language of inclusion—statements that use "we" or otherwise express a shared identity and purpose—engages a process in which we convey to others that we believe they are reliable and trustworthy. Inclusive language ties us psychologically to other people by defining us as members of some common group (the organization, a department, a project team). It helps us and others to see that our fates are intermingled, that we depend upon one another. In turn, this felt interdependence helps us to see others as reliable, their behavior as predictable and their intent as benevolent, and to act accordingly.

To work this way, however, inclusive language must be authentic both in intent and impact. Above all, it must agree with our actions. If I use "we" as a signal that I trust and depend on you, but other aspects of my behavior negate this sense of our common fate, trust is broken. Every time trust is broken, it takes much more energy to restore it to the same level than it did to build trust in the first place.

The potent effect of inclusive language on trust is especially apparent when we use it to share credit with others. So much work in organizations is collaborative work. Even work that looks solitary often is not. As I noted in the Chapter Three, it's often an invisible army of people who enable us to accomplish what we do each day. Yet people vary a great deal in how much they include others in talking about responsibility for tasks being completed and successes being achieved. Sharing credit for work done through the use of inclusive language is one of those small connecting moves that carry a lot of punch with lasting impact. It honors and invites connection. It sends a message we will trust and depend upon others in the future. In a similar way, failing to use inclusive language when its use is expected, warranted, and hoped for can be devastating, chipping away at potential future trust between two people.

Trusting By What We Don't Say
We convey trust by what we refrain from saying as well as by what we say. If we say things to others that communicate negative expectations of their integrity, dependability, or benevolence, we instantly destroy possibilities for trust.

Not Accusing of Bad Intent. As I have noted, a key part of building trust is conveying a belief in others' honesty and the benevolence of their motives. Unfortunately, we often receive bad or incomplete information about another person's intent or circumstances. Jumping to conclusions that someone didn't have good intentions is one of the surest ways to damage the future trajectory of a relationship, making it very difficult to rebuild a sense of trust.

Suppose that in the story of Zena and Joe that opened this chapter, Zena had received incomplete information and that Joe's unit had forbidden him to tell her about the marketing plan he was developing until the plan was revealed. The apparent breach of trust could have been healed by a trusting act on Zena's part. Instead of deciding that Joe must have acted in bad faith, she could have discussed her disappointment with him and invited him to explain what had gone on from his point of view. By refraining from accusing him of bad intent until all the facts were known, she would have left the door open to a healthy and trusting connection. In fact, if Joe then grasped how things must have seemed to her, he would be likely to see her invitation to talk as a powerful statement of trust.

Not Demeaning Others. In Chapter Two, I noted how common disrespectful engagement is. This means that words that undermine the worth of others are common currency in many places. Words that demean others shatter the foundations of trust. They make people afraid and defensive. They contradict the trust-building message that we rely on others to meet our expectations.

Demeaning others can be a control move, and asserting control and holding onto power cripple rather than enable trust. As a surgical intern, Angeline Smith worked with an attending surgeon who was known for his spectacular skills. His patients all liked him. But he was a classic type: civil and caring to those above and beside him in the organizational hierarchy but demeaning in his treatment of those below him. He was condescending to interns and greeted their questions with cruel half-jokes like "Are you sure you went to med school?" This made them afraid and unwilling to ask questions. In short, his style conveyed a lack of trust, and in turn the people who worked under him were distrustful and insecure. This breakdown in trust undermined Angeline's capacity to learn and the surgeon's ability to pass on his knowledge. The competence of the organization as a whole was diminished by small acts that blocked rather than opened up quality connections.

Trusting By What We Do
Beyond our words, our actions can powerfully convey trust and invite others to trust us. The behaviors discussed in this section are particularly rich ways of building trust.

Giving Away Control. We signal trust when we delegate decisions and tasks, especially when doing so means we must rely on others to bring about results that affect our own fate. Subordinates see delegation of tasks to them as a sign that their boss has faith in their choices and trusts they will make decisions that are good for other people and for the organization as a whole.

Managers, of course, delegate work every day. The tough question is whether to give away control and responsibility when it really counts—when the future of an idea or product is on the line. Such acts of trust can inspire others to excel in order to meet our expectations, as in this story related by a senior manager in a large consulting firm: "I gave a junior team member the task of making a proposal presentation to a prospective client. Not being fully aware of his abilities, I took a risk; it took some trust. It was a long shot. However, the junior team member was highly motivated and did a lot of work in preparation for the event. He made a great presentation, and we got the contract. He actually exceeded my expectations and hopes. It took a leap of faith on my part."[13]

One of my former students, Steve Mondry, who is currently an investment banking analyst at Deloitte & Touche, describes how he is motivated to perform when his managers convey trust in him by asking him to do tasks that represent the company: "For example, managers here often ask me what I think we should do when we hit a tough spot in a deal. They may ask me to call a client and explain why I think we should be doing something our way and not their way. By asking me to call the client rather than calling themselves, managers allow me to represent them and the firm in client discussions. This makes me feel like I am a decision maker and not just a human calculator. It also motivates me to perform better and learn more."

A particularly powerful example of how giving away control and responsibility can build trust and enable connection comes from Will Adler, head of strategic planning at Timberland. Will told the story of being responsible for taking groups of urban youths on challenging outdoor adventures to enjoy the splendor of the wilderness and to learn about themselves in the process. On one of the final summer trips he boarded the bus to begin the mountain trek with what appeared to be an unruly, tough group of kids. The ring leader was Derek, the physically biggest and oldest kid and a Bloods gang member. Derek wasted no time asserting his physical dominance on the bus. There was a turning point moment when Will faced the choice of whether to use heavy-handed control to show Derek who was in charge. Remembering advice he had received from his mentor, Will took an unexpected action. Instead of trying to assert control, he gave it away by giving Derek the power and responsibility to lead the boys. In Will's words:

> I sat and talked to Derek for five minutes or so on that bus. I told him I saw two options: one, he goes home. Or two, he helps me lead. He looked at me like I was crazy, but seemed interested. I told him I saw a leader. And I asked him if he had ever been given the outlet to lead. He said no. I told him he seemed comfortable in charge, he agreed. I told him that he had the opportunity to make a real difference in the lives of those kids. By settling them down and tuning them in to the wilderness experience, he could be responsible for changing their lives.

The results of this trusting act were quite remarkable. Again, in Will's words:

> We walked off the bus and my staff had the students all set to go. We didn't announce anything, Derek just asserted himself as the sort of spiritual leader that day. I ran the logistics. Derek kept the group in order: "Act right, and listen up—this is one of the most incredible places you all may see. Being here could change you." He was projecting his own experiences, and like wildfire his serious enthusiasm spread throughout the group.

Derek handled himself and the wilderness with dignity and modeled those values on the kids. He kept the kids in line throughout the day and under his tutelage they remained safe and experienced some life-affirming moments.

This example has many parallels in work organizations, where through countless small moves we signal our belief (or lack of it) that others will act in good faith. I am constantly reminded of how subtly I communicate lack of trust in some of my students by being too controlling or not giving them adequate responsibility. By not trusting boldly, as Will did with Derek, we may miss the opportunity to help someone grow toward their own greatness, to the benefit of all.

Giving Access to Valuable Resources. Another way to convey trust is to put resources in the hands of others. The more valuable the resource, the stronger the trusting signal. Sometimes the sharing of valuable resources involves providing access to material goods, other times it involves emotional resources (like support) or attentional resources (like time) that signal a trusting act.
   Markus Vodosek, a faculty member at the University of Michigan Business School, has studied more than a hundred chemistry research groups; he finds that the way group members treat resources (lab equipment, preparations of chemical compounds, physical lab space) is a powerful signal that creates or destroys trust in a flash. The ongoing assumption is that other lab members will "take care of the stuff," meaning that they will use the resources well, ensure their availability for others, and not tamper with equipment and materials that might jeopardize the experiments of other people. Vodosek finds that even small offenses such as taking another lab member's stirrer without asking or leaving a moldy sandwich on a lab bench can lead to a deep sense of distrust. He saw major differences across lab groups in terms of how members convey trust in each other by opening or closing access to the most valuable resources.

In our everyday work lives we routinely make decisions about what resources to put in the hands of others. We do this by direct giving of resources but also by granting access to resources. By granting access I mean actively removing barriers for people to get to the resources they need to get their work done. Granting access implies giving freedom to an individual or group to use data, people, systems, or other valuable resources as they need them. Such actions build trust because people see them as an acknowledgment that you believe they will use the access well. For example, when I hand over the key to my office or to my house to someone I am working with, or when I give my administrative assistant my computer password for file access or my credit card for travel billing, I am granting access to resources that could be used to hurt rather than help me. These granting moves are trust activators because they signal my belief that someone is reliable and trustworthy.

Granting access is often a keystone of building effective interorganizational partnerships. For example, Cyndie Bender, CEO of Meridian Travel, builds high-quality relationships with customers by doing extensive information sharing with them. Against the backdrop of an industry that runs with lots of suspicion, she operates with an open-book policy. She routinely shows clients the full set of expenses, costs, and profits on the full range of items in their service contracts (including flights and hotel bookings). They know how much it costs Meridian to serve their needs. The open-book policy signals that Meridian trusts its customers to act in good faith. In Cyndie's mind this is what makes the relationships between Meridian and its customers flourish.[14]

Soliciting and Acting on Input. Sincerely soliciting others' input is a powerful way to build trust. When you seek the input of others, you demonstrate your trust in their competence. In return, you gain from their advice and enhance the trust between you and them.

One manager I talked to routinely solicits input from his subordinates by asking them to put themselves in his shoes: "You can contribute in new ways, you can do some parts of this job better than I can, I need your views on this matter. What would you do if you were in my place?"

Not only does seeking counsel convey faith in others, it also builds trust by exposing one's own vulnerability. As trust expert Dale Zand suggests, when people accept counsel from others, "they increase their potential for harm in several ways. They may be seen as weak, as not doing their job, at the same time that they could be misdirected."[15] In addition, a genuine request for counsel or feedback is a form of giving away control, because we don't know what the counsel will turn out to be.

The act of accepting what we hear can be a further powerful boost to trust. Bob Holmes, former director of human development at the University of Michigan, tells a story about how one of his assistants was brave enough to give him feedback that suggested he was not behaving in line with the value of trust that he was trying to convey in the unit. While his initial reaction to the feedback was resistance, upon reflection he realized she was correct: he had, in fact, not been acting in a trusting way. He nominated her for a staff award as "departmental truth teller." Not only did this act of trusting and rewarding trusting bolster the quality of his connection with her, it signaled to the whole group that he was serious about their role in helping him honor his talk about trusting. The quality of the connections he had with other members of the department was taken up a notch.

Of course, an even more powerful way to convey trust is not merely to solicit input but to act on it. Acting on others' input sends a powerful message of faith in them while at the same time enhancing others' trust in our sincerity. At Muhlenberg Medical Center in Plainfield, New Jersey, management was in the middle of changing a command-and-control culture to one that was open and empowered. As part of this change, more and more employees at various levels were being listened to as a way to create a different performance culture and to improve the hospital's effectiveness. One highly successful endeavor involved converting charity care for the hospital into a profitable enterprise. Rhonda Owens, one of three clerks in the hospital who won the bid for the approach to dealing with charity care, describes how her manager's response to input inspired trust: "It was not just the fact that Janet listened; it was also that she acted—immediately. When I told Janet an idea I had, she said, 'Great idea,' and she moved right on it. It's not like when you tell somebody something, and then you never hear about it again. With Janet, the next day it's done."[16]

As a final example, a project manager I know explained at her retirement dinner why she had lasted for more than fifteen years in her job and loved every minute of it. She recalled that on her first day of work her boss handed her a series of project files. He told her to go through them and come up with a set of ideas. If they sounded good, he promised to support her in implementing them. He supported the very first project she proposed, and together they succeeded in implementing it. In retrospect she marveled about how trusted and supported she felt, and how that initial experience set a trajectory of success. The story reminds us that acts of trust at the beginning of a relationship can go a long way toward establishing the quality of the connection that develops.

Trusting By What We Don't Do

As with words, the behaviors we refrain from are just as important as the things we do in building or destroying trust. Trust is fragile. Once broken, it is hard to repair. This section discusses two types of actions and practices to avoid as you work to build trust.

Avoiding Check-Up Behaviors and Surveillance. One sure-fire trust torpedo is to "entrust" someone with a task and then check up and see whether the person is delivering. The more monitoring and checking mechanisms we put into place to make sure that someone is doing things the way that we want, the less trusted they will feel. Moreover, surveillance and checking mechanisms make it hard for people to demonstrate that they did something because they felt trusted. There is always the rival explanation that they did it because if they did not, they would be caught and suffer some kind of consequences.

Sociologist Brian Uzzi did a wonderful study of the way garment firms do business in the New York apparel industry.[17] He documented the competitive success associated with more trusting relationships between people both within and across firms. He found that if managers in the garment firms had more trusting relationships with managers in other firms, it gave them more flexibility to access resources and more opportunity to co-operate, which contributed to the firm's overall competitive success. Trusting relationships were distinguished, in part, by the absence of monitoring devices. In the more trusting relationships, people invested more in trying to solve problems as they came up, there was more passage of useful information between firms, all facilitating the firm's ability to adapt to changing competitive conditions. Thus Uzzi's study is a reminder that the same factors that are important to trusting within organizations also contribute to advantages across organizational boundaries.

Refraining from resorting to monitoring and checking devices can mean acting without the safety nets that are so often routine in organizations. For example, when I give presentations that depend on the presence and quality of input from other people, I have a choice: I can count on them to pull their weight and deliver, or I can prepare backup plans and other measures just in case they don't. As more and more of my work becomes interdependent with others, the latter choice of preventive preparation creates an impossible workload for me. At the same time, I am learning that it undermines my team members' sense that I trust them. I know I am on the path of building a high-quality connection when I do not do the just-in-case preparations. However, I find that to be trusting in this way takes effort. It means suspending doubt and training myself out of the "always being in control" and "cover myself or else" beliefs that were inculcated in the early part of my career.

Avoiding Punishing People for Errors. Trusting a person or a group to do what is right means not punishing them when they do something that doesn't work—something wrong. Trusting means betting on the person and the person's efforts. Sometimes the efforts will translate immediately into better-than-desired results. At other times the results will fall short, but you can be sure the effort will be greater than if the trust were not there in the first place.

It is particularly shortsighted to punish people for taking risks simply because their decisions do not produce the desired result. Taking some risks is crucial both for personal growth and organizational success. Punishing risk taking because the results were disappointing does not encourage better decisions, it only discourages taking any risks at all.

Another form of punishment to avoid is publicly chastising people for poor performance. This type of humiliating behavior can be seen by some as part of "being tough"; they think of it as "necessary" and an important part of playing "competitive hardball," but it is also a guaranteed trust killer. My colleague Peter Frost writes about pain in organizations and the ways that people play roles of mopping up and absorbing the pain caused by others' cruel and inappropriate behavior.[18] Publicly demeaning or humiliating someone, or showcasing faults and failures, is toxic behavior. It poisons the ground of trust not only for the person who is chastised but for everyone who witnesses or hears of the event.

■ Challenges to Trust

As with all connecting pathways, it is easier to describe trusting actions than to do them. Trust can feel risky and dangerous. Some of the challenges to trust are specific to the particular connection or relationship. Thus how you work with the challenge has to be customized to the history and nature of the relationship.

Challenge #1: Bad History and Past Disappointments

It can be easier to behave in a trusting way if we are beginning a relationship anew. A new subordinate, boss, customer, or coworker connects to us based on a clean sheet with no disappointments to cloud our expectations. If, however, we have a bad history with another person at work, it takes active, sincere, and mutual effort to repair the damage. Trust violations "rend the fabric of the relationship and, like 'reweaving,' they are expensive and time-consuming to repair, such that the fabric may never look quite the same."[19] Here are some possible actions to consider in beginning the repair process:

- *Communicate your experience of the trusting failure with the person who violated your trust.* Behavior will not change unless the other person knows damage has been done, and specifically what actions caused this damage. This type of communication works best if it is done in a straightforward and respectful way. Recall the earlier advice about not accusing others of bad intent. Describe how the person's behavior affected you without imputing bad motives to that individual.

- *Communicate your willingness to let the other person earn back your trust.* To build a high-quality connection, you must give another person an informed second chance by communicating that your trust has been violated, but that there is a chance for your trust to be restored if the individual acts in a way that honors that trusting endowment.

Sometimes the attempt at repair simply does not work. It is important to know when it is time to quit and to effectively end the expectation that trust can be built. While signposts that trust is impossible are never clear-cut, it is important to have established a standard or threshold that, if met or crossed, means that the other person cannot be trusted, and the relationship will never achieve higher quality. In this case, you may choose to communicate the crossing of this line to the other person, making any future attempts to build trust unlikely.

Challenge #2: The Terror of Giving Away Control

Most of us are afraid of giving control to others—often the heart of trusting—because we are afraid of the consequences. We fear that if we give up control things will fall apart, a situation will get worse, or that the future will become more uncertain. As Bob Knowles, plant manager at DuPont's Belle plant, asks: "If you leave behind control by directives, dictating results and outcomes, how do you keep things from falling apart and losing focus?"[20] Here are some steps that start to deal with this challenge:

- *Start small.* Experiment with trusting. This week, try delegating a task or responsibility that you have not yet given away. It does not have to be a large or high-risk delegation. To convince yourself of the connecting potential from trusting, try experimenting with delegating something less risky. Practice not monitoring or checking up on the person.

- *Pay attention to the yield the experiment generates.* Notice and tune in to the value of your acts of trusting. Be sure to seek feedback to learn from this experiment in giving away control. How did your subordinates read your delegation of responsibility? What did it mean to them? Also compare what actually happened with the anxiety or fear you might have felt in making a trusting move. Were your worries borne out? Or were you rewarded by your act of trust?

Challenge #3: Misestimating Others' Sense That We Trust Them

Our interactions with others are often fraught with perceptual errors. This is especially true of the assumptions we make about trust. Research suggests that we often overestimate how trustworthy we are in the eyes of others, and that at the same time we assume others are less trustworthy than they actually are.[21] These double-barreled misperceptions make organizational relationships breeding grounds for mistrust rather than trust. Here are steps you can take to surface hidden assumptions and correct perceptual errors about trust:

- *Ask people you work with how they see your trusting behavior.* Do not assume that their perceptions match what you think you've communicated by your trusting behaviors, or that your behaviors match what you believe about their trustworthiness. Have reality check conversations with colleagues to see whether they feel as trusted as you mean for them to feel.
- *Actively seek others' suggestions about how to improve the accuracy and effectiveness of the signals you send about trust.* Ask colleagues which of your behaviors they find most potent in signaling your trust or lack of trust in them. (Recall that soliciting feedback and being open to change based on what you hear is itself a powerful trust-building move.)

Challenge #4: Personal Trust and Attachment Styles

For some, trusting others at work and activating this virtuous cycle of relationship building comes easily. For others, trusting another person is demanding and emotionally taxing. Individual differences can make it easier or more difficult to trust another human being. For example, psychologists have uncovered differences in what they call "attachment styles" that affect people's willingness and ability to trust others. *Attachment styles* are the mental representations that we have of others and ourselves that organize our thoughts, feelings, and behavior in relationships. Attachment theory suggests that these styles are formed every early in life and that they affect the kinds of emotions we experience when trusting, the kinds of meanings we attach to trust, and the kinds of reactions we have to trusting.[22] In particular, people with a *secure* attachment style feel more comfortable with interdependence and closeness and are more confident about others' feelings toward them. Trusting others is easier and more pleasurable for people with that sort of attachment style. In contrast, people with an *avoidant* style, as the name denotes, experience much more fear about closeness and interdependence. They experience insecurity about others' intentions and so prefer to maintain some distance between themselves and others. As one might expect, for people who have learned an avoidant style, trusting others is often difficult and painful. Finally, people who have an *anxious-ambivalent* style want closeness but are insecure about others' responses. This style, too, can make it difficult to trust others.[23]

Although research suggests it is difficult to change these basic attachment styles, being aware of them helps to make sense of our own experience of the ease or difficulty in using trust as a pathway for building connection. The concept of attachment styles also may help us understand others' behavior and the challenges they experience in using this relationship path.

- *Explore your own history of trusting.* What has enabled or disabled your trusting of others in the past? What are your default assumptions about most people's trustworthiness? Awareness of your own default assumptions about others' trustworthiness will help you to be more conscious of how much or how little someone will have to do to earn your trust.
- *Try revealing your trust assumptions to a person you want to build a high-quality connection with.* Help the other person to understand your personal situation (your goals, your concerns) and a bit of your history so as to read your trusting signals with a fuller and more authentic sense of what is behind them. Invite the person to reciprocate by sharing personal goals, concerns, and history with you. Remember that appropriate self-disclosure itself helps to build trust.

■ Putting Trust to Work

Energizing your workplace by building connections based on trust takes work. Begin by taking stock of the current role of trust in your work relationships. To this end, two assessments are provided in this section. The first assessment asks you to reflect on how people are using trust to build connections with you. The second assessment invites you to consider your own trusting behavior and what you might like to do differently in the future.

Recognizing Trust Investments from Others

Exhibit 4.1 invites you to list and think about the individuals and groups you see as trusting you. The goal of these reflections is to provide a different angle on the "trust bank" that exists for you in your current work organization. If the trust bank is well endowed, indicating that many individuals and groups trust you, then you have great resources to draw upon in building and sus-

Exhibit 4.1. Mapping Trust Investments from Others

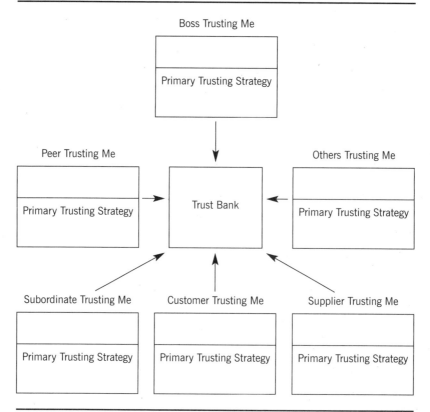

taining high-quality connections. Moreover, just as a solid bank account can fund many things you would like to have or do, trust investments are wonderful assets—they generate flexibility, freedom, resourcefulness, and security. If, on the other hand, you find that your trust bank is less well endowed than you would like, it is time to consider action to encourage trust investments.

Step 1

Who trusts you? Identify individuals you think currently trust you. Be sure to consider systematically people who are in various positions relative to you (bosses, subordinates, peers, customers, and suppliers). Choose one member of each group who typifies a person who trusts you and write their name in the top of the box. Use the "Other" box in Exhibit 4.1 to identify persons that trust you at work but who do not fit neatly into any one of these categories.

Step 2
Identify the primary strategy that each trusting individual is using to convey their trust in you. Do people or groups seem to be using similar strategies of communicating that they trust you? If there is a pattern in their strategies, what does it say about how you elicit trust from others? Are there actions that you might want to take to increase or alter strategies that others use to convey trust in you?

Step 3
Consider the distribution of trust. Do you have the trust investments that you desire and need? Are there people or groups you did not identify as currently trusting you that you would like to add to the picture? Are you surprised by any of the groups or individuals who showed up as currently trusting you?

Assessing Your Trusting Investments in Others

Once you have assessed others' trust investments in you, you're likely to appreciate more than before how much you are enabled and energized by trust. Now take a more focused look at your own patterns of trusting to see where you might want to change, strengthen, or weaken your trusting actions as steps toward building high-quality connections. Exhibit 4.2 provides a worksheet for this exercise.

Step 1
Identify your closest contacts at work. In Exhibit 4.2, list the names of peers, subordinates, bosses, and customers you interact with the most. You can list individuals or you can list groups.

Exhibit 4.2. Analyzing Your Trusting Investments

Trusting Behaviors

	Talk		Actions	
	Say	**Don't Say**	**Do**	**Don't Do**
	Sharing information Self-disclosure Telling others about trusting	Accusing of bad intent Making demeaning comments	Giving away control and responsibility Giving access to resources Soliciting and accepting counsel	Monitoring and checking Punishing errors
Close Peers				
1.				
2.				
3.				
4.				
Close Subordinates				
1.				
2.				
3.				
4.				
Close Bosses				
1.				
2.				
3.				
4.				
Close Customers				
1.				
2.				
3.				
4.				

Step 2

For each person or group you have listed, consider the degree to which you are currently in trusting mode by what you are saying (and not saying) and what you are doing and not doing. Exhibit 4.2 lists the specific trusting behaviors discussed in this chapter, but you may do other things as well. List them. This analysis makes very concrete how your behavior is creating a trusting pattern that meets or does not meet your connecting goals.

Step 3

Look for patterns in your connections and trusting behaviors. Looking across the relationships you've listed, where are your trusting investments heavy? Where are they light? Does this investment pattern reflect your desired goals for building connections with others? Are there techniques that you are using to convey trust in one relationship that you might want to apply to another? Assuming that you feel a high degree of trust in someone, are you using the full range of ways to convey your trust to that person or group?

Step 4

Analyze the means that you are using to make your trusting investments. Are they working? What are the benefits? If they are not working as well as you would like, can you try others?

CHAPTER SUMMARY

The third pathway for building high-quality connections is trust. Trusting means acting toward others in a way that conveys your belief in their integrity, dependability and good motives. Positive words and actions that create trust include sharing valuable information, appropriate self-disclosure, using inclusive language, giving away control and responsibility, granting access to valuable resources, and soliciting and acting on input. We also create trust by the things we do *not* do or say, including accusing others of bad intent, demeaning others, check-up behaviors and surveillance, and punishing people for errors.

Among the challenges we confront in using trust to build connection are having a bad history with another person, the terror of giving away control, misestimating others' trust in us, and attachment styles that may make it difficult to trust others. The chapter offered several suggestions for dealing with these challenges. Finally, two assessments were presented to help you explore your "trust bank" (the investments of trust that others have made in you) and your own patterns of trusting behavior.

Dealing with Corrosive Connections

So far this book has focused on how to build high-quality connections with others at work—connections that energize, that are life-giving. Unfortunately, the starting point is not always relationships that are benign or neutral. Some connections at work are life-depleting. They undermine our sense of trust. They eat away at our sense of dignity and respect; they disable us, making us feel less rather than more competent to do what we have to do. I call these kinds of connections *corrosive* to emphasize their caustic effect on our well-being and functioning. My colleague Peter Frost labels them *toxic* because of the damage they do to the health and vitality of individuals and entire work organizations. Whatever we call them, if we are concerned with the impact of the quality of relationships on ourselves and our organizations, then we need a way of identifying, understanding, and dealing with corrosive connections.

Corrosive connections are brought about by behaving in ways that are directly opposed to the pathways for building high-quality connections discussed in the preceding chapters. Such actions are everyday occurrences in most work organizations. Some corrosive acts are ambiguous, making it difficult to decipher the intent of the other person, but others clearly display negative intentions. Whether ambiguous or unambiguous in intent, corrosive acts have the same damaging effects. They hurt. They drain energy. As one manager said, "They take the life right out of you." Ultimately they create connections that wear us down. Listen to one employee describing the impact a corrosive connection with a colleague had on her: "My emotional reaction was disbelief that this coworker could continue to lie [to the media] . . . about our 'shared project.' Our relationship is strained to say the least. I find this to be an extremely emotional experience which causes me doubt, weariness and stress."[1]

Typically instigators of corrosive connections have more power than their partners in the relationship.[2] Corrosive connections with those in authority or with power over you can be particularly damaging, as in this example of public humiliation of an employee at a large bank describing the actions of his boss: "I was angry—felt humiliated and betrayed. [I] felt like I had been stabbed in the back with no way to defend myself or explain my position. [Because of the audience] . . . I probably would not have confronted the senior management person in this meeting even if time permitted. . . . He forever damaged my credibility. I never trusted him again."[3]

Often, corrosive behavior may be an offshoot of a flexing of power, and the offending party may be oblivious to the damage that ensues. As I noted earlier, people in higher-status, higher-power positions simply do not pay as much attention to those below them as people in lower-status positions pay to those above them. Consequently, people in higher-power or status positions may find it difficult to see their causal role in creating corrosiveness, and they may be less motivated to remedy this destructive pattern. For this reason it is often the person with less power who must notice the corrosiveness of the relationship and take action to deal with it.

In this chapter I first describe the variety of corrosive connections that occur at work and their effects on individuals, work units, and organizations. Then I identify a range of strategies for dealing with these destructive connections. Some of these strategies are designed to create a buffer that can mitigate the hurt, pain, and emotional fatigue that accompany being in these kinds of relationships. Others provide means of beginning to transform corrosive connections into higher-quality, energy-creating connections.

As a manager, you may consider these strategies from two vantage points. First, you can use the strategies when you find yourself wrestling with what to do in a corrosive connection with a peer, subordinate, or boss. Second, you may find the strategies useful in coaching employees who find themselves in corrosive connections.

■ Corrosive Connections at Work

You can take action to deal with corrosive connections only if you recognize them and the damage they are doing. Thus it helps to be acutely aware of the variety of forms such connections take and the dynamics of their corrosiveness.

Corrosiveness in Everyday Encounters

Corrosive connections are created and sustained by an infinite variety of disrespectful, disabling, untrusting, alienating acts—in short, by behaviors that are the opposite of the pathways to high-quality connections.

I have already described a number of examples of such acts in preceding chapters. As I have emphasized, these behaviors need not be big, damaging actions. It is often the small digs and displays of inattentiveness at work that are most lethal. Chris Pearson and her colleagues, who have studied incivility at work for several years, call these small corrosive acts the "incivilities of working life."[4] Here is a brief reminder of their many colors.

Disrespectful Engagement

Disrespect eats away at a person's energy and sense of felt worth. Disrespectful engagement can be quite direct, taking the form of degrading verbal slashes from a colleague, customer, or, as in this case, a boss: "What did I tell you the first day? Your thoughts are nothing, you are nothing. . . . If you were in my toilet bowl I would not bother flushing it. My bath mat means more to me than you, you don't like it here, leave!"[5] But everyday corrosion can also be subtle and indirect, as in this story of utter thoughtlessness someone told me: "I rushed into my boss's office to tell her of the birth of my new niece. She looked up from her work for only a couple of seconds and said, 'That's nice.' She didn't ask me questions. She did not show any emotion. This event marked the point at which I gave up on forming a connection with that woman."

Disabling and Task Disruption

Actions, or failures to act, that make it difficult for others to get their work done create corrosiveness. For example, it can be highly destructive to the quality of a connection when people who have crucial information or resources (whether material or emotional) choose not to share them. Regina Krain talks about a boss who withheld critical support at crunch time: "I was dealing with all this, and did not get support from my boss like I should have. She said she could help me do things. I can remember exactly. I needed help getting things typed and stuff and she went for an hour's break. And that was very negative. . . . That's probably one of the most negative experiences I had [in this department]. I wasn't feeling supported."[6]

Similarly, failing to respond to feedback on an issue that bears on someone's ability to work effectively corrodes a connection. Josh Smalley, a member of the computer support staff at a pharmaceutical firm, described his experience to me this way: "I tried to talk to my boss about it before. It just goes in one ear and out the other. There are still lots of problems, and she's not listening to what needs to be addressed. . . . It's been frustrating all the way. . . . You know, it makes you feel like you're talking to a brick wall. . . . I'm feeling a little overwhelmed . . . because I have other things to be dealing with."

False Promises and Acts of Distrust
False promises and acts that display a lack of trust are sure pathways for building corrosive connections. Listen to a former MBA student describing her boss on an internship. In between the lines in the example is her sense of having an implied contract broken. When she interviewed for this internship and decided to take it, Brian (her prospective boss) promised to invest heavily in her development. However, he never went beyond the bare minimum in delivering on that promise. "Brian used 'by the book' development meetings with me. During these meetings he would provide me with copies of presentations and speeches on topics such as leadership and vision. His communication was one-way, formal, and mechanistic as he explained the material. I listened. There was absolutely no dialogue. I always had the feeling that these meetings were his way of checking off a little box requiring managers to develop interns."

It's no surprise that when offered the job at the end of her internship, she turned it down, having had a taste of the corrosive, life-depleting possibilities of being "developed" by this manager.

The Destructive Dynamics of Corrosive Connections

As the examples presented so far illustrate, corrosive connections deplete individuals' energy and motivation. However, the damage does not stop there. The corrosiveness in a relationship can seep into other parts of the organization, melting and damaging connections beyond the starting point. Two examples of destructive spirals illustrate the damage done by unchecked corrosiveness.

Spirals of Incivility

Incivility rarely stays contained. It spirals and spreads within the work organization's boundaries at the same time that it spreads and spirals into people's lives outside work. This spiraling effect happens for several reasons. First, word spreads because bystanders sometimes witness corrosive behavior. Second, people who are hurt and angered by uncivil acts often need to talk about it. In one study of the experiences of more than twelve thousand people who encountered incivility in the workplace, virtually every target of incivility described telling someone else about the experience.[7] When news of incivility spreads it increases people's expectations that these behaviors are normal, further increasing their occurrence. A third reason spirals happen is that the targets of corrosive behavior sometimes displace the negative emotion and stress on someone else—subordinates, customers, even family and friends.

The Death Spiral: Turning Competent Performers Into Basket Cases

When people are caught in corrosive relationships, they often blame themselves and question their own competence and efficacy. Corrosion thus erodes self-esteem and masks talent with insecurity and self-doubt. These self-doubts can start a death spiral of loss of confidence and competence. Here is how one former MBA student described her experience of a death spiral: "Jennifer, my manager, did not trust me. She didn't trust my comments in meetings and she didn't trust the overall quality of my work. I know she didn't mean to hurt me. She was acting like a responsible manager would—she was concerned about us giving the best quality work for our client. I could respect that. But unfortunately, the constant checking and lack of trust created a 'death spiral.' As she approached me, I became nervous, my work movements became slower and less confident and eventually, plain and simple I just messed up!"

■ Strategies for Dealing with Corrosive Connections

Given the damage that corrosive connections do, it is important to confront these toxic relationships. In this section I discuss five strategies for dealing with corrosive relationships. The first two are immediate actions that help reduce the pain that comes from being in a corrosive connection. The final three are longer-term strategies that typically involve greater investments of resources for dealing with the corrosive connection.

Although they're all imperfect, each strategy opens new possibilities for action. The key is to avoid letting yourself become merely a victim, which only magnifies the effects of negative connections. Action is better than no action. The grips of corrosive connection are much tighter and more damaging if you believe there is nothing you can do about them. As a manager who is being vigilant about signs of corrosiveness in connections between people who work for you, you can play a critical role in naming this issue and offering coaching on various ways for dealing with the situation.

Naming the Problem

Work organizations can make it very difficult for people to express negative emotions that indicate pain, stress, and dissatisfaction.[8] As a result, the tendency might be to repress the anger,

disgust, humiliation, and disappointment associated with these
corrosive connections. However, suppressing negative emotion
can do more harm than expressing it. The challenge is how to
express the emotion in a way that promotes healing.[9]

Naming the problem is one way of expressing and releasing
negative emotion. Simply identifying the emotions you are feeling can help you gain perspective on how a situation is affecting
you. Similarly, naming a connection as corrosive or abusive can
help you begin to develop a framework for understanding the
emotional dynamics of the relationship.[10] Moreover, giving the situation a name normalizes the experience by implying that you
are not alone: others, too, experience this kind of pain. As one
manager suggested, "If I call a spade a spade [label the relationship as being as bad as it is] I feel less alone. It's out there and
something to tackle, as opposed to inside, eating away at my
sense of hope and worth."

Creating a Sense of Control

Once you have named the problem, it is helpful to create or
maintain some sense of control over the corrosive situation.
Sometimes this means setting goals, even small ones, that can
create a sense of accomplishment within the restricted space of
a corrosive connection. For example, Laura Hale, a senior public affairs specialist, explained how she deals with a very toxic
boss. While she can't reduce the amount of contact and work interdependence with this person, she makes a game out of trying
to make her boss smile or display other signs of warmth during
the day. When she gets a "warmth sign," she celebrates. In this
small way she regains some sense of control.

Once you have named the problem and refused to be powerless about it, you can turn to more active strategies for dealing
with a corrosive connection and its life-depleting effects. Of the
remaining three sets of strategies, the first two are intended to

limit the damage caused by the connection. The final set aims at transforming the connection itself.

Bound and Buffer

"Bound and buffer" strategies involve erecting psychological barriers that minimize the impact of being in a corrosive relationship. While these strategies don't alter the connection at its heart, they do reduce the damage it does by limiting psychological exposure to the life-depleting relationship.

Reducing Interdependence and Reliance on the Other
One effective strategy for dealing with a corrosive connection is to reduce the level of task interdependence. Simply put, this strategy means limiting how much a corrosive connection can affect you by reducing your reliance on the other person.

This strategy can take the form of a mental game of "who needs this person?" This helps you to see that your reliance on the other person is less than you imagined, allowing you to mentally distance your fate from the other person's. Unfortunately, untying the knot mentally is often impossible. You and the other person may genuinely be interdependent in the work setting, so that your fate does get tied up with the fate of the other party. In these situations it may be worth the effort to reduce your level of task interdependence with the corrosive partner. For example, Peggy Shields is a fast-track middle manager who has run into a brick wall: her new boss, who won't make time for her and has given her no sense of expectations, goals for the division, or input regarding basic necessities like budget, customer prospect lists, and so on. There has been no response to her requests to meet. Even though she is stuck with him as her boss, she is taking three measures to reduce the level of interdependence and so limit the corrosiveness created by what she experiences as an uncaring and unprofessional response.

First, she makes an effort to meet and build connections with her boss's peers. This move gives her alternative paths for getting key information and builds an alternative network for support. This has proved easier than she expected because of the opportunity to sit together at lunches and the physical architecture of corporate headquarters, which facilitates casual interactions. Second, she has been doing extensive research about the new market she will be serving, thereby reducing her need to rely on her boss for information. Finally, she is using other networks to find out how her boss operates, what he values, what his "hot buttons" are. This intelligence reduces her reliance on personal interaction with him to discover and work with (and around) his preferences and points of sensitivity.

Psychological Disengagement

The ability to hold oneself apart from a corrosive relationship— to disengage psychologically—is an important option when people find themselves in destructive relationships that they cannot escape. Disengagement can mean removing oneself physically from the source of corrosiveness. For example, resilient survivors of troubled family situations often successfully disengage from the grips of their families by getting jobs, volunteering, playing sports, or actively engaging in legitimate activities that take them away from the corrosive home scene.[11] At work, of course, this type of leaving the scene can be tough to pull off. Two coping strategies that may be more viable are "armoring" (creating psychological buffers) and social withdrawal.

The term *armoring* has been used to describe adaptive ways that people cope with racial oppression.[12] Armoring implies creating ways of thinking that put up a psychological shield, keeping hurts and fears from doing major damage to how we think about ourselves. Naming the destructive relationship is a part of armoring, as is building up one's own strengths (as discussed under "Buttress and Strengthen," later in this chapter). Armoring can also involve using humor as a means of acknowledging the reality of the corrosive situation while turning it into something that is more distant and objectified, thereby reducing its sting. Some people regularly read "Dilbert" jokes for the comic relief they provide from the sometimes absurd situations imposed on people at work. The popularity of "Dilbert" is a testimony both to its accuracy in portraying what people recognize as hurtful and destructive conditions and to their ability to distance themselves from those conditions and laugh at them.

When corrosive connections are too destructive, and it seems like nothing is left to be done, it may be necessary to resort to *social withdrawal*. Becoming "invisible" can help insulate you from harmful attacks or other undermining behavior on the part of people you work with. Accounts of political corrosive behavior in organizations document the frequency that people use this "keeping my head down" strategy.[13] Concretely, this form of coping may involve not participating in informal get-togethers or discretionary activities that take you into face-to-face contact with the person with whom you have the corrosive connection.

Buttress and Strengthen

We open a new set of options if we consider how to buttress and strengthen ourselves as a way of dealing with corrosive connections. These options do nothing to actually change the relationship, but they do build up our own endurance and resilience, so that over time we gain the energy and fortitude for deploying other strategies for dealing directly with the corrosive connections themselves.

Strengthening One's Own Resources
There are a number of ways to strengthen your internal resources for dealing with a corrosive situation. Peter Frost, an expert on dealing with toxic emotions at work, suggests increasing

self-protective resources by strengthening four main areas of life: physical, emotional, mental, and spiritual.[14]

For example, Frost suggests meditation and breathing exercises as important ways to regenerate. He also suggests creating personal space or ways to leave the press of the stressful connection and finding a mental or physical sanctuary where you can rejuvenate. John Bergez, the wonderful editor who has enabled me with this book, has a routine that exemplifies this form of strengthening practice: Each day he tries to designate a space and time when he literally physically leaves work for a short period. He uses the discipline of imagining himself crossing a line or a boundary (sometimes marked graphically by cracks in the sidewalk). At the line's crossing, he stops, counts to ten, and imagines dropping the load of whatever is on his mind like baggage left behind. The line's crossing is treated as moving into a sacred space where nothing is allowed to intrude. He then walks for fifteen to thirty minutes, consciously directing his attention to something other than the roots of the stress, noticing surroundings, focusing on details, reciting a poem to himself, or simply letting his mind empty. Although he has been using this process for some time, he notes that it takes continual practice because worries or stressors are persistent, and seem to work hard to reinvade his mind even in these short interludes. However, when he succeeds in creating this "sacred" space, the effects are palpable. He continues to be amazed at how rejuvenated he feels. His story is a reminder that these forms of strengthening practices are small moves that can make a big difference, particularly if we do them regularly.

Constructing a More Positive Self-Image
Often we turn a corrosive situation on ourselves by viewing an interaction as affirmation of our own weaknesses or shortcomings. In reality, we may be the target of someone else's hurtful behavior, yet our self-image suffers in a way that can be very

damaging. An important buttressing and strengthening strategy, therefore, involves taking stock of ourselves and constructing our self-image in as positive a light as possible. The word *constructing* is important because it emphasizes that we have a hand in building our self-view. People who are resilient in the face of adversity don't get bogged down with blame or with trying to fix impossible situations. Through positive self-perception and self-talk, they turn the adversity into a form of challenge that yields positive insights about themselves and helps them recognize personal strengths.

Seeing yourself this way does not mean being blind to your own weaknesses and faults. It means actively reminding yourself of evidence that, in fact, you *are* a worthy person. My daughter Emily gave me a great example of this coping strategy. She told me about a tactic she uses with the few teachers she has had who seemed a bit cruel and self-serving. She obviously can't exit the relationship with a teacher. However, she describes how she tries to make sure that she remembers that she is a different person from the one she feels like in this connection. She conjures up real counter facts to her teacher's sent message. For example, she recalls more positive feedback that she has gotten from other teachers, or she focuses on particular projects that she has done in the past where the outcome made her very proud. She talks to herself to say that she is smart, that she is talented, and that this teacher simply can't see her for who she is. Positive self-talk like this can help to write over the negative self-construals that form in a corrosive relationship.

Another example of deployment of this same strategy involves deliberately collecting appreciative letters, e-mail messages, and notes that represent concrete and specific evidence that what you have done in the past is worthwhile and valued. Sometimes people keep these in a file. My collection is all electronic under the "favorites" tab. Such a file is the repository of raw materials that can be used to bolster your image of yourself, when it has been dwindled or tainted by the actions of corrosive relationships at work. The self we see is partially what others reflect back to us and partially what we project to the world. In the face of corrosive relationships at work, we are strengthened by actively seeing and projecting our positive attributes and strengths, as an alternative picture to the negative portrait reflected by a hurtful and damaging connection.

You can even turn your effort to cope with a corrosive relationship into a source of positive self-knowledge about your competence and strength. For example, here is an example from research on individual resilience that shows how this can work. The speaker, a young adult, describes the satisfaction she achieved from coping with highly destructive family dynamics. In essence, she turns corrosive connections with her family into a source of satisfaction for dealing with a really tough situation: "Don't get me wrong. Managing in my family was no joy ride. Asserting myself was not like the fun you have by buying something new, going to a movie, spending time with someone you like or taking a luxurious vacation. Those pleasures are simple— relatively easy to come by. The kind of satisfaction I got from handling problems in my family was far more complicated and mixed with pain. There was always a build-up and release of tension. It was a matter of seeing what I could do for myself."[15]

Seeking Insight

Corrosive relationships do damage in part by seeming to come out of nowhere, leading us to feel that they are our own fault. Accordingly, one way to strengthen your capacity to deal with these connections at work is to invest effort in arriving at a correct understanding of them. By understanding the root causes of corrosive behavior and the situations that may elicit it, you are better able to predict when such behavior is likely to occur, to avoid blaming yourself, and to know what you might do to protect yourself. In studies of how people survive and eventually thrive in abusive homes (the ultimate in corrosive situations), researchers Steven and Sybil Wolin call this means of building resilience "insight."[16]

You can seek insight in a number of ways. One involves using frameworks or ways of understanding the corrosive situation that help you to see its meaning in a new light. For example, one of my neighbors works at a software development firm that, like most start-ups, is cash-constrained and disorganized, putting everyone under immense stress. The situation has become quite political, with everyone vying for a slice of the reduced pie. My neighbor has started reading a book called *Of Wolves and Men* that describes the behavior of wolf packs.[17] In her judgment, understanding her colleagues' actions by analogy with the behavior of a wolf pack gives her a fresh perspective on what she is dealing with and helps her identify new possibilities for action. She saw that her colleagues were acting in beastly ways, more predatory as a group than she would have expected based on knowing the individuals. As a result of this insight my neighbor was able to identify new possible motives for their action, as well as ways to respond that were more effective. For example, she intentionally started meeting more often with individuals in the group on a personal, one-on-one basis, and rarely interacted with them as a group (or a pack). This way of dealing with them actually reduced her sense of the impossibility of the situation, and helped her to see ways of intervening with individuals on a one-on-one basis to make life less difficult.

Seeking insight does not have to be a solitary act. Talking to friends, family members, and sometimes colleagues can uncover new possibilities for understanding the causes and effects of the life-depleting connection. In the example of Peggy Shields, she consulted with me, with other friends, and with a well-trusted colleague, actively seeking different ways of seeing the situation and what she could learn from it. These inquiries have helped her see that her new boss's overly controlling ways are part of his need to establish his own authority. While this insight does not change the objective situation, understanding the source of his behavior makes living with it more tolerable and suggests possible ways to interact with the boss that might diminish his controlling behavior in the future.

Finding Positive Meaning in the Connection

A different form of buttressing and strengthening involves seeking out positive ways to see the corrosive connection itself. This does not mean denying its corrosiveness. It means thinking about how the connection is less hurtful than it might seem and could even be beneficial in ways that might not be readily apparent. For example, you may see a difficult relationship with a colleague as an opportunity to strengthen your own competence at speaking up or your ability to understand difficult people. You might view it as a type of endurance test that you are in fact surviving. Or you may take a comparative stance and see that compared to other people in your unit, you are actually better off than most, or that the relationship isn't as bad as corrosive connections you have endured at work or elsewhere in the past.

Research has shown that small changes in the degree to which people find positive meaning in negative events can actually improve their long-term physiological well-being and health.[18] In addition, finding positive meaning in negative events has been shown to increase people's coping resources and ability to bounce back from setbacks. In psychology there is growing interest in interventions called "benefit finding," which are constructive practices for people dealing with unchangeable negative events in their lives. Benefit finding works partially by cultivating more positive emotions, which in turn bring about changes that allow people to deal more effectively with events in the future. For example, if individuals can see positive meaning in learning to cope with a difficult employee, it may produce a sense of pride and heightened self-efficacy that emboldens them to imagine better outcomes in the future. The research on benefit finding suggests that looking for the positive meaning in a corrosive connection is a viable strengthening strategy.[19]

Altering One's Sense of Time

Another mental strategy that can provide calm and increase your resolve and strength involves changing your sense of the duration of your corrosive experience. Although the experience of pain often feels like an eternity, you can remind yourself that the experience started not that long ago, or that it will end not that long from now. For example, Elliot Smith, a longtime mortgage lender, deals with lots of corrosive relationships with clients. He has devised a simple and effective strategy for coping with the pain. He simply reminds himself that when he puts time in the right perspective, the corrosion is just a short endurance test. He has a large paperweight that he uses to remind himself that his struggle is time bound. The paperweight is an ancient chunk of amber. The amber reminds him to calibrate time by using a much longer horizon. When he does this, the weeks he has dealt with a particularly tough client start to look like an eye blink in time instead of an eon. The panic that comes with dealing with a corrosive customer loses some of its edge that way, and he is able to get back on a more even keel.

Finding Hope and Tapping into Optimism

Hope and optimism are strong defenders against the physiological and psychological damage of being in a tough corrosive connection. Studies of mental and physical health offer stunning evidence that both optimism and hope heal. Although the exact way that they work remains a bit of a mystery, it's clear that people who face adversity with positive expectations about a better future and a more optimistic explanatory style are better able to adapt. Optimists tend to stay more problem-focused in the face of adversity, have an easier time accepting the reality of situations, and tend to see the positive meaning in the event ("I am learn-ing to be tough," "This is really testing my ability to get along with people," "I am learning to deal with tough customers by dealing effectively with my tough colleagues").[20]

Hope "reflects the belief that one can find pathways to the goals one is seeking and become motivated to use those path-ways."[21] It is associated with positive emotions and thoughts. When we are faced with corrosive relationships at work, adopt-ing a hopeful, optimistic perspective encourages us to actively consider many ways to deal with the relationship, to set goals for dealing with it constructively, to take credit for any progress we make, and to see the situation, rather than ourselves, as re-sponsible for setbacks or lack of progress. Hopefulness and op-timism don't come naturally to everyone, so it may be necessary to work at cultivating these attitudes.

Building Supportive Relationships

Positive connections with others can serve as important antidotes to the corrosive relationships that we cannot escape at work. Sup-portive connections buffer the stress and anxiety associated with corrosive relationships. They provide safe harbors where we can rebuild our sense of worth and dignity. They provide vital sus-tenance and emotional nourishment to sustain us in the midst of corrosive connections at work. Being aware of the restorative ca-pacity of these relationships is critical to buttressing ourselves against the wear and drain of corrosive connections. We all have many options for building these kinds of restorative connections, but we may need to think creatively about the possibilities. Here are several.

First, find a particular individual with whom you feel es-pecially safe and affirmed, whether a fellow employee or some-one outside of your immediate work environment. Sometimes organizations facilitate access to these kinds of connections through mentoring programs or other means of matching employees with people who can foster their developmental success. Other times, you are on your own in building this kind of restorative connection. One key is to look for someone who can assist you in thinking about and dealing with the situation, not just provide a sympathetic ear. For example, it is especially useful to connect with individuals who may have a fresh perspective or who can suggest new practices for dealing with a particular type of corrosive relationship.

Second, join or start a group within the organization that can be a safe harbor and replenishing haven for you. Sometimes you may find that such groups already exist. For example, as part of its diversity effort, General Motors has created self-governing affinity groups, modeled after similar groups at IBM, SBC Communications, and General Mills that are intended to be sources of support for individuals who may feel isolated and alone. One goal of the affinity groups is to create a context in which members with shared backgrounds and characteristics (for example, the Hispanic affinity group, the gay and lesbian affinity group) can trust, connect with, and learn from one another.

You can also think creatively about building a support group inside your organization. Here's an account of one such group created by women in an accounting firm: "Eight women sit around a boardroom table over lunch in a Boston public accounting firm. These are the busiest of women, in middle- and senior-level positions from inside the accounting firm and from a mix of nonprofit organizations and large corporations. All of them are mothers with young children. They juggle the demands of their work, children and homes. Some of the women travel on a regular basis in the United States and overseas, yet they all make time to attend one of Jane's biweekly lunchtime Perspective, Renewal and Balance (PRB) meetings."[22]

Third, consider participating in professional associations or other work-affiliated groups outside the organization. These kinds of groups can really make a difference in sustaining you

in the wake of corrosive connections. For example, two colleagues, Connie Gersick and Jean Bartunek, and I have studied
the importance of relationships in academic lives. We learned
that many people say that their professional associations are
"lifelines." Associations and their affiliated meetings provide
critical information and networking opportunities that reduce
members' reliance on their local contexts, offering important opportunities for escape, replenishment, and renewal.[23] Professional associations also offer knowledge communities and
opportunities to learn how to deal with the dilemmas of corrosive relationships that may be particularly endemic to your type
of job or occupation.

Fourth, explore other outside groups that create safe
havens for emotional venting, emotional support, and problem
solving for dealing with corrosive connections. Vicki Parker, a
researcher for the Department of Veterans' Affairs,[24] calls these
connections "GROWS," which stands for Growth-enhancing Relationships Outside Work. GROWS can be vital sources of information and feedback that help you cope with challenges at
work. For example, people often rely on their families, on civic,
community, and service groups, and on religious organizations
to rejuvenate them emotionally when they are facing tough
work relationships, as well as to provide perspective and advice.

If you cannot find the right kind of safe harbor or support
group outside your work organization, think about creating one
for yourself. For example, Carla Jones was a rising star in facil-
ity management at the Port Authority of New York and New Jersey. She was thriving at work, but she had occasional run-ins
with old-time transportation executives who seemed to be un-
comfortable with her management style and rapid career success. She wrestled with several corrosive connections at work,
but saw no safe way to talk about them in the workplace. For a
while she employed a therapist to help her strategize and deal
with these challenging work connections. Although it was strate-

gically helpful, the therapy work did not resolve the sense of aloneness she felt in this upward battle in a male-dominated organization. Five years ago, she got together with five other working mothers in her hometown and formed what came to be called WPAG (Working Parents Action Group). Meeting once a month at night in a local church, this group became a developmental sanctuary that helped her deal emotionally and instrumentally with the challenges of the corrosive connections she experienced at work.[25] But it did much more. It created a political action group that worked toward changes in their town to make it a more hospitable environment for working parents. It became an emergency back-up child care system for helping members deal with the uncertainty and anxiety of child care dilemmas. It served as a safe harbor to vent anxiety and frustrations about the challenge of dealing with a high-power job and a young family.

As this example suggests, healthy, life-giving connections, whether inside or outside the organization, can help people hold onto identities and core values that may be challenged in corrosive connections. Deb Meyerson and Maureen Scully studied how people make organizational change happen even when their identities and values depart from the dominant ideology inside their work organizations.[26] They found that people who do this successfully rely on developing relationships with people that sustain them during the difficult change process. Meyerson, in her book *Tempered Radicals,* suggests that forming supportive affiliations, both inside and outside the organization, was the number one way that the change agents she studied held onto their sense of self.[27]

Target and Transform

This last strategy for dealing with corrosive relationships involves more work and more personal risk in the short term than the other two, but is more likely to change the corrosiveness of the connection because it involves altering the nature of the re-lationship itself.

To illustrate how the strategy works, I will draw from a single case of a corrosive connection.[28]

Mary Hanes and Ken Vaughn were both experienced design engineers working for Tidewater Corporation, a manufacturer of luxury power boats. For some time Ken had seemed on the edge of an emotional explosion. When he berated Mary in front of their colleagues about a new product design that she had worked on for months, Mary lost two nights' sleep tossing and turning as she thought about the incident. It seemed so unlike Ken. They had been colleagues for years, and had shared personal and professional triumphs together. The relationship that used to bring her great energy and pleasure had turned sour, and now the two were barely speaking to each other. She had resorted to buying packets of Tums (a common antacid tablet) both on her way to and from work. Mary was very concerned about approaching Ken, yet she knew that something had to change as her own physical health was starting to suffer from being in this toxic connection.

When a connection becomes so corrosive that it begins to do major damage to our own well-being or health, and strategies for enduring the corrosiveness aren't enough, then the "target and transform" option deserves consideration. To "target and transform" means to make the relationship itself a matter of explicit concern and attempt to change the nature of the connection. This strategy can be appropriate for any corrosive connection—it's not just a last-resort measure. It is designed to alter the foundation conditions of the connection by changing the way one or both parties act in the relationship. It does this through a process of *respectful negotiation*.

The idea behind this strategy is that we can learn a great deal about how to repair a corrosive connection from people who do negotiation for a living. In the case of dealing with corrosive connections, respectful negotiation means working with the other person to change the way you are interacting with each other with the mutual goal of repairing and transforming the connection.

This kind of process intervention is tough. It requires a giant change in perspective with regard to what is going on, a leap of faith that says that if we engage the process of interaction with a different kind of paradigm in our heads and our hearts, we can turn things around. I recognize the difficulty in accomplishing this kind of shift, particularly if shards of hurt, anger, and disillusionment are left from previous toxic interactions. Yet the same can be true of difficult negotiations, which often involve lengthy histories and painful emotions. It is just for this reason that the idea of respectful negotiation is helpful as we think about how to repair and transform corrosive connections.

Deborah Kolb and Judith Williams, two negotiation experts, suggest that successful negotiations require that people simultaneously be good advocates (making clear and compelling what they need and want) and good connectors (doing real relationship building).[29] Their perspective provides useful insights for how we might convert corrosive connections into neutral—and even better, energizing—connections. A negotiation approach to transforming corrosiveness in a relationship involves four concrete steps.

Step 1: Clarify Your Own Needs
A negotiation mindset requires being clear about what we want out of a connection. Knowing what we want helps us to avoid getting pulled into the destructive dynamics of disrespectful engagement, name calling, or any of the millions

of other ways that people can spiral into corrosive interactions. It is also helpful to know what needs or interests we most want to protect or meet as we renegotiate the terms of our connection.

In the past Mary had had a sense that Ken valued their relationship, but they had never explicitly talked about what each of them needed or desired in this work connection. As Mary tries to rebuild her connection with Ken, she needs to be very clear that, for her, the primary goal of the relationship is to effectively collaborate to continue to produce top-of-the-line designs for Tidewater Corporation. In addition, Mary has the goal that she and Ken continue to be positive role models for other design engineers who are members of Tidewater. Finally, Mary wants to continue to have social contact with Ken in the form of their monthly tennis games. Keeping these needs in sight will help her keep her approach to Ken properly aimed. It will also help her affirm to herself and to Ken that her needs are legitimate.

As Kolb and Williams suggest, this is a critical part of the preparation process. "You must convince yourself that your demands are legitimate and believe you have the right and the ability to push for them."[30]

Step 2: Seek Information About the Other's Needs
Successful transformation of a connection through negotiation also means moving the relationship in a direction that takes account of the other person's needs. Preparation for the transformation must therefore involve a realistic and meaningful assessment of the other person's needs.

Mary decides to do two things to help uncover and focus on Ken's needs before she approaches him to begin the negotiation process. First, she pauses to take stock and think through past interactions and conversations to derive a more explicit listing of what she thinks Ken has enjoyed and required in their connection. Taking stock helps her to realize that Ken had demonstrated earlier difficulties in asking for help if he was overloaded. However, she also remembers that he took help when it was offered in ways that allowed him to retain his expert status. Next, she asks other colleagues for their impressions of his needs for connection generally, and in particular, with respect to his relationship to her. She is surprised at how these steps help her see more options for what she and Ken might change in their interaction patterns to make it more of a win-win.

Step 3: Think Through Alternatives

In negotiation language, thinking through alternatives means knowing your BATNA (Best Alternative to a Negotiated Agreement).[31]

For Mary, developing her BATNA means thinking through in advance what will she do if she and Ken cannot come to an agreement about how they will interact in the future. For example, she needs to consider whether she has alternatives to relying on Ken for getting the collaborative engineering work done. Similarly, she needs to consider alternatives to Ken for positive role models for the other engineers. Consideration of alternatives also means considering worst-case scenarios.[32] For Mary and Ken, the worst case may mean a deteriorating connection, where the corrosiveness increases. Thinking this scenario through may help Mary uncover an additional set of alternatives to have ready at hand in their negotiation. For example, she may want to complete research on local consultants who could be hired on a temporary basis to provide direct help to ease the load on Ken. The consultant option may allow Ken to preserve face, while at the same time building capacity in the system to meet the immediate deadline.

Thinking through alternatives also involves considering how to demonstrate that the other party has something to gain from changing the status quo. We are all aware of people who seem to have no sense about a need to change a poisonous relationship.

One of Mary's challenges is to motivate Ken to consider changing the way he interacts with her. Negotiation theory suggests that he must, first, see some value to their interactions, and, second, have an interest in change. The bottom line is that he must see that Mary has something to offer him if he changes his behavior.

This "carrot" approach will not work with people who see no value in what the other party has to offer. In such a case, the individual affected by a corrosive relationship may need to resort to legal or other formal means to try to alter the corrosive behavior.

Mary, however, believes that Ken does value their connection and is not fully aware of the damage he is doing to it. She thinks one way to motivate him is to make clear the effects that his behavior is having on her personally and on their working relationship.

Step 4: Negotiate

Only after the preparatory work in the first three steps is it time to proceed to the final step of actually negotiating. By *negotiating* I mean, in this context, engaging in collaborative dialogue to come to a new understanding about actions needed to improve the corrosive situation. Kolb and Williams offer sound advice that could be productively applied to Mary and Ken's situation, as well as situations you may face. In the negotiation process they recommend:

- *Take steps toward building or restoring connection.* Engage some of the connecting strategies discussed in preceding chapters: being present, being affirmative, actively listening, responding through supportive communication, enabling the other person, conveying trust.
- *Encourage participation.* During the process make sure both people are getting a chance to speak and check to see if people are feeling heard. These kinds of process checks should help to ensure that both people are fully involved and on the same page in terms of assumptions and a sense of where the dialogue is going.
- *Work to ensure joint ownership of the process of restoring and transforming the connection.* Encourage a sense of mutual responsibility for its current and desired quality. The steps taken up to this point should help to establish this spirit of mutuality. In addition, try to win agreement on needs and goals that you both share. State your own goals clearly and listen carefully to those of your partner. Use the skills you've learned in earlier chapters, such as staying objective and checking to see that you are hearing the other person accurately. Strive to create a process and agreement that represent the work of both people.
- *Seek formal corrective action.* A totally different line of tactics involves using a formal grievance process, or formally reporting the corrosion in some way that activates the organization to intercede to remedy the situation. In rare cases this remedy will involve removing the corrosive partner. In most cases, it will activate a more formal inquiry, some documentation of the facts, and some form of mediation to try to improve the relationship in some form.

■ Putting the Strategies to Work

I hope that this chapter has convinced you that corrosive connections are worth dealing with—whether that involves limiting their damaging effects through bound and buffer strategies, buttressing and strengthening your own endurance and resilience, or working to transform the connection itself. As in earlier chapters, I invite you to assess whether you have considered the full array of options you have at your disposal.

Exhibit 5.1 summarizes the strategies presented in this chapter. You can use this tool when you are confronted with a corrosive connection yourself and as a guide for coaching someone you are working with who is caught in a corrosive connection.

Begin by asking whether you have the will and means to change the corrosiveness in the relationship. If yes, skip to the target and transform strategy. If no, consider whether a bound and buffer strategy or a buttress and strengthen strategy is a better place to begin. The important point is to start wherever you can make progress either in changing the connection or stopping the drain of energy and life that it is causing.

Where none of these strategies are sufficient and you see no possibility for transforming the connection, it can be appropriate to consider more formal means for corrective action or, as a last resort, leaving the unit or organization. Too often, though, people either suffer corrosiveness passively or jump to the conclusion that there is nothing to be done except to leave. When confronted with a corrosive connection, you owe it to yourself to make a serious effort to change the situation or control its effects. After such an effort, many situations that seemed hopeless can be made tolerable and even become occasions for personal and professional growth.

Exhibit 5.1. **Strategies for Dealing with Corrosive Connections at Work**

Naming the Problem

- Identify the emotions you feel and their source in the connection.

Creating Some Sense of Control

- Set small goals to help you see some sense of accomplishment (remember, small wins matter).

Bounding and Buffering Strategies

- Consider ways to reduce your interdependence and reliance on the other person. (Think creatively!)
- Consider ways to disengage psychologically, including armoring and social withdrawal.

Buttressing and Strengthening Strategies

- Consider ways to strengthen your own stock of resources.
- Actively work to construct a positive self-image.
- Seek insight into the causes and dynamics of this connection. Consider alternative ways to think about the relationship dynamics using different frameworks and ways of seeing it.
- Find positive meaning in the connection.
- Try to make the connection endurable by altering your sense of time—how long the situation has been going on and when it will end.
- Tap into sources of optimism and hope.
- Build supportive relationships with individuals or groups inside or outside your work organization.

Targeting and Transforming Strategies

- Treat the process of changing the relationship as a respectful negotiation.
- If your own efforts fail, consider requesting an outside intervention or, as a last resort, leaving the situation.

CHAPTER SUMMARY

Corrosiveness in connections is manifested in a variety of ways, often involving small, everyday actions that drain and dispirit. Once corrosion begins, its destructive dynamics lead to a gradual worsening of the situation and to wider and wider effects within the organization.

Several types of strategies can help in dealing constructively with corrosive connections. As a manager, you may find them useful both in dealing with situations you confront personally and in coaching others who are wrestling with corrosive connections at work.

Two immediate strategies include naming the problem and gaining some sense of control. Beyond these, three longer-term clusters of strategies can help minimize the damage done by a corrosive connection or change the connection itself. Bounding and buffering strategies focus on limiting the physical and emotional harm the connection is causing by reducing levels of work interdependence and psychologically disengaging from the other person. Buttressing and strengthening strategies focus on building up one's own endurance and resilience. They include strengthening your physical, emotional, mental, and spiritual resources, constructing a more positive self-image, seeking insight into the connection, finding positive meaning in the connection, cultivating optimism and hope, and building supportive relationships with individuals or groups. Finally, the targeting and transforming strategy focuses on turning a corrosive connection into a healthier, higher-quality connection by engaging in a process of respectful negotiation.

When none of these strategies produce the desired result, it may be necessary to seek formal corrective action or to leave the situation. We owe it to ourselves and to our organizations, however, to do what we can to deal with a corrosive situation constructively before deciding that we are powerless to change it.

Building High-Quality Connections in Your Organization

I hope by now you are convinced that high-quality connections are as essential to your organization's energy, well-being, and performance as they are to your own. That means they have special meaning for you as a manager, because you have a greater degree of responsibility than the average employee for the overall excellence of your unit and organization. As a manager, you are an architect of context. What qualities, then, would you try to create in your unit and organization in order to foster high-quality connections? And how would you go about it? This final chapter addresses these questions.[1]

■ Cracking the Code: Organizational Contexts That Enable High-Quality Connecting

The organizational context makes a big difference for the ease and lasting impact of efforts we make as individuals to build high-quality connections. Work organizations are the organisms in which our micro moves to build connection take place. The same move (being open with a boss, helping a colleague, protecting or supporting a subordinate) can have stronger or weaker connecting effects in different organizational settings. The question is, how can you contribute to making your organization one that encourages everyday high-quality connections and maximizes their impact? If you could start from scratch, what features would you build into the organizational context to make high-quality connections more likely to be created and sustained?

You might think of answering these questions as a code-cracking exercise akin to mapping the human genome. It implies analyzing the rich and diverse set of clues implicit in organizational contexts to uncover the code that governs the way the organization develops and functions. Knowing the code gives you starting points for knowing what to cultivate and what to nourish to build a context that is energized, vibrant, and highly functioning because of its rich supply of high-quality connections.

In the following sections, I discuss seven sets of clues that I have found to be associated with a greater likelihood of high-quality connections. I then turn to how you can put this information to work to improve the context in which you work.

Clue 1: Culture and the Power of Values

Shared values are the bedrock of any organization. Strip away the strategy and structure of an organization, and at its core you will find its values. Values are what people in an organization believe to be good, worthwhile, and important. They are created and sustained by the organization's leadership, its rewards, and the types of people that it recruits and promotes.

We often know the values in an organization by the consequences that follow action. For example if the talk is about teams, but the rewards (formal and informal) are based on individual performance, then good team behavior is not likely a living value in the organization.

What values are conducive to employees' building high-quality connections in units, in teams, across levels and across organizational boundaries? Is there a set of organizational values that are likely to foster high-quality connections? My research suggests at least four such values. And though all four need not be present for high-quality connections to flourish, each one makes them more probable and more lasting.

Valuing Teamwork

An organization that values teamwork sees collective responsibility and collective action as worthwhile and good. Team values orient people to care for the performance and fate of team members who are participating in doing some part of the work of the organization. At AES Corporation, one of the largest independent electric power producers in the world, teams are not only the norm for organizing but a part of the firm's core values.[2] Task force teams take care of all the regular and ad hoc functions necessary to do electric power production around the world: water treatment, maintenance, auditing, safety, and so on. The valuing of teamwork keeps people directed toward learning and helping each other. Teamwork as value and a structure built on teams work together to fuel the creation and sustenance of high-quality relationships.

Valuing the Development of People

Some work organizations see developing and growing their employees as a central and worthy activity. Organizations with this value foster practices whereby people are encouraged and enabled to achieve their potential and reach their career goals. Valuing the development of people means more than facilitating each individual's career achievements, however. At a more profound level, it means a belief in and shared commitment to playing an active, positive role in facilitating the personal growth and development of each individual.

At St. Luke's of London, sometimes called the ad agency to end all ad agencies, people assume "Everyone is brilliant" and "It's a matter of finding their place and allowing them to reach their potential."[3] At VeriFone, growing people and growing the business go hand in hand. Katherine Fines, a senior manager of VeriFone, states the value this way: "We are striving to achieve respect for every individual for what they can bring to the table."[4] When a commitment to affirming people and fostering their development is part of an organization's way of life, high-quality relationships flourish as people are engaged by their hearts as well as their heads. The valuing of development encourages the expression of what each individual cares about and needs, at the same time that it implies that efforts will be made to enable people to work toward and satisfy these needs. Research shows that in these conditions, people act more authentically.[5] And when people act authentically, they can connect to each other on a more lasting and secure basis.

Valuing the Whole Person
The third value is a natural companion to the second. In some organizations you can bring your whole self to work, and some organizations make you want to hide or tuck away pieces of yourself that the organization sees as work-inappropriate. Where the organization values the whole person, people have latitude to be more fully present, more authentic and less afraid to reveal who they really are. All these conditions create fertile ground for building high-quality connections.

At the business school where I am employed, I am constantly reminded that the whole person matters. I take this context for granted until I go to another part of the university or to other business schools, when I am stunned by the sharp boundaries drawn between what is and what is not appropriate to include in your work life. For example, the valuing of the whole person is enacted in the way the school treats people's families. For MBA students this message is conveyed in the way their families are included in recruiting events and in the everyday life of the students while they are here. The Spouses of Students organization (which includes partners of students as well as spouses), is one of the most vibrant student organizations; it is involved in raising money, sponsoring and organizing events, and serving as an information source, central networking agency, and sponsor for serving diverse student needs (jobs, child care, and so on). For most faculty the experience is similar: having a family (extended or otherwise) is seen as normal, and acting to preserve family is valued. This aspect of the culture is communicated by the inclusion of families in events, the policy that faculty meetings end by 5 P.M. so that people can attend to child care needs, a vibrant annual family picnic, and the posting of pictures of the picnic in the hallways for weeks after the event. Each of these practices etches more deeply the value that employees are whole persons who are supported in honoring their other life commitments.

In addition, the normalcy of talking about hobbies, vacations, illnesses, and fuller life circumstances in everyday conversations expresses and strengthens these values, creating a positive loop whereby the values that sustain life-giving relationships at work are themselves strengthened by the connections that develop. Bob Shapiro, former CEO of Monsanto, talks about how caring connections breed valuing of the whole person: "If you are working with people who really care about each other, they have an interest in your being healthy, in your being whole. They don't want you to be there every night until eleven o'clock. Doing that for long periods of time, it's not going to work for you."[6]

Valuing Respect and the Dignity of Others
Organizational cultures vary in how much they value the worth and dignity of every individual regardless of rank or position. Organizations that value everyday respect and the dignity of each employee protect the baseline conditions for effective relationships that in turn enable the effective conduct of work.

In studies of two very different organizational contexts, surgical-care units in hospitals and cross-functional groups involved in airline departures, management researcher Jody Gittell found that in organizations where mutual respect was valued, employees had a much easier time achieving the coordination necessary to produce high-quality products and services. Mutual respect allowed people to rely on each other and to react in an authentic and timely way to the emerging demands that were natural but nonroutine parts of both the surgical and flight departure processes.

Contrast the way employees at two airlines spoke about the organizational context in which they worked. In the airline where respect was central people talked one way about their colleagues: "No one takes the job of another for granted. The skycap is just as critical as the pilot. You can always count on the guy standing there. No one department is more important than another." In the airline where mutual respect was less central, people talked this way: "There are employees working here who think they are better than other employees. Gate and ticket agents think they're better than the ramp. The ramp think they're better than cabin cleaners, think it's a sissy's women's job. Then the cabin cleaners look down on the building cleaners. The mechanics think the ramp agents are a bunch of luggage handlers."[7]

How much does all this matter for organizations? In the book *Good to Great*, which describes why some organizations are able to turn into sustainably excellent companies, Jim Collins and his collaborators uncovered an interesting finding: companies that went from good to great were marked by collegial relationships that often lasted for life.[8] Making everyday respect a priority converted connections into lasting mutual regard that built and sustained people's connection to the company as well. Dick Appert of Kimberly-Clark put it this way: "I never had anyone in Kimberly-Clark in all my forty-one years say anything unkind to me. I thank God the day I was hired because I've been associated with wonderful people. Good, good people who respected and admired one another."[9]

Collins concludes, "The people we interviewed from the good-to-great companies clearly loved what they did largely because they loved who they did it with."[10] A culture of mutual respect and dignity sets the stage for this form of high-quality connecting.

Clue 2: The Design of Rewards and Recognition

As I noted in the discussion of values, reward systems—formal and informal—either undermine or affirm the values that foster high-quality connections. They create the awareness and the feedback that put values into action. For example, network expert Wayne Baker claims that the most important lever for affecting the social capital of an organization involves the design of incentive systems.[11] If incentives are not set up to foster linkages, then high-quality connections are limited.

Two features of formal reward and recognition systems are particularly diagnostic. First, are rewards based on collective as well as individual performance? Collective incentives support values such as team accomplishment. For example, valuing teamwork becomes a reality when employees are substantively rewarded based on team performance. Nucor, one of the world's most successful steel companies, has a pay scheme whereby steelworkers have more than 50 percent of their compensation tied to the work teams of which they are members.[12] Collective rewards create motivation to treat team members with respect and dignity. Over time, they may foster trust. They create the reality of shared fate that binds people together in constructive ways.

Second, are people rewarded for developing and enabling others? This type of reward scheme provides fuel for building and sustaining high-quality connections. For example, in some 360-degree performance evaluation reviews, not only do subordinates get to rate their bosses and provide feedback, they are encouraged to document and rate how much their boss has helped them to achieve their own goals for the performance time period. These kinds of reward processes facilitate high-quality connections and speed individual and collective learning by building in incentives to enable and help each other. When the reward systems also permit noticing and rewarding coworkers for enabling each other, this feature of the context becomes an even more powerful facilitator of connection. For example, Southwest Airlines motivates this kind of helping by having "agent of the month awards" where fellow employees choose winners. The whole performance system is designed to reward behavior that facilitates high-quality connections, which in turn are an important part of the explanation for the airline's sustained competitive success.[13]

Beyond formal rewards and recognition, informal rewards and recognition practices are also useful clues. Organizations (and leaders) tip their hands on the value they give to relationships by their choices of people to thank and the way they thank them. Some organizations facilitate genuine expressions of gratefulness and thanks for contributions to the organization or to other employees' personal output and performance. Sadly, too many organizations wait until formal retirement occasions to publicly declare someone's value to others. Others may arrange occasional recognition events, but only a few make frequent recognition of employees' contributions a regular and normal part of doing business. A good question to ask when trying to assess your own organization is, Do those who contribute from the back office get the sincere kudos they deserve? Consistently?[14]

The business school where I work has a highly successful staff recognition program. All employees can participate by nominating people to receive one of the prestigious awards that are given twice each year. Beyond the $500 cash prize, a picture in the staff newsletter, and a plaque, the winners are publicly recognized in a valued ceremony. Snippets from the letters of nomination are read, and all nominees are given copies of their nomination letters. This program is a living testament to the fact that staff is vital to the whole organization.

Clue 3: Structure, the Division of Labor, and the Power of Networks

All organizations rely on a division of labor in order to get things done. Whether an organization makes steel, heals patients, or provides knowledge consulting, the work requires some division and specialization. These divisions can work for or against the building of high-quality connections.

High-quality connections are disabled when divisions are unnecessary and when they are about granting power and status as opposed to allowing useful specialization and economies of scale. Dividing and layering in organizations can create unnecessary inequalities that separate people, making it difficult to build life-giving connections. As I noted earlier, high-quality connections thrive in contexts of mutuality. Thus another indicator that an organization is well suited for building high-quality connections is limited layers and hierarchy. Nucor, for example, uses a variety of measures to keep class divisions and separations between its organizational members at a minimum.[15]

First, the structure is flat: only four layers separate top from bottom. Second, executives have few privileges not offered to nonmanagers. Some perks are even offered to employees alone. For example, employees have access to $2,000 per child per year for post–high school education, a benefit that is not available to executives. There is no executive dining room. Symbolic differences are also minimized. Nucor's annual report lists all seven thousand employees' names instead of the usual practice of listing only company officers and members of high-ranked boards.

Whereas hierarchical and vertical distinctions are structural features that make high-quality connections tougher, networks and ties that connect individuals and groups work in the opposite way. Ties are the links that we forge with other people by knowing and interacting with them. We can know them well, communicating lots and feeling a sense of emotional closeness (strong ties), or we can know people slightly, having much more casual and distant connections (weak ties). The patterns of ties that we have with others are called *social networks*. Where people are linked through more ties in a unit or organization, the connective tissue of the whole is better prepared for building high-quality connections. These kinds of networks build a sense of mutual obligation and shared experience among employees, enabling knowledge sharing and strengthening the quality of the connective tissue between people.[16]

Two features of the organization's networks are helpful clues. First, networks are more conducive to high-quality connections when they are characterized by "optimism and positive attributions regarding the formation of new relations."[17] These characteristics are more likely when people in the networks know each other, trust each other, and have had affirming experiences in the past with members of the networks.[18] Second, networks foster high-quality connections when people in the network are tied to each other for multiple reasons. In the words of network scholars, the ties are *multiplex,* meaning people are connected to each other through multiple pathways. For example, I might know my colleagues as work partners, but also may be tied through friendship and through shared hobbies. This richer means of connection implies the organization has more avenues for building high-quality connections.

Organizations vary considerably in the level and type of networks shared by their employees and the nature of the ties that members have with customers and other important partners. A powerful example of the difference that networks can make in building a vibrant connective tissue linking all players participating in producing a critical product comes from, Holiday Elementary School, an exemplary educational organization in a very challenging environment.[19] The school is situated amid public housing projects on Chicago's West Side, and two-thirds of its 550 elementary and middle school students are from the public housing projects. Holiday Elementary School is thriving, as are its students, despite these challenging circumstances. A major reason for this success is that teachers, staff, and students are interconnected through multiple network ties. The school's leadership has played a proactive role in facilitating frequent communication among staff, teachers, and parents. Parents, teachers, and staff have collaborated to create demanding and supportive classrooms and they have worked outside the classroom to make the environment safe for all who spend time there. Through working together on many types of projects in service of schools, they have created multiplex ties where people have high expectations about one another's contribution to the educational mission. Trust and mutual regard pass through the veins of these vibrant connections between people who are participating in the education of the children. The multiple ties create excellent circuitry for communicating and an effective means for adjusting quickly to changes in circumstances affecting individual students or the school as a whole.

Clue 4: Practices and Processes for Getting Things Done

The established practices and processes by which an organization accomplishes basic tasks equip and motivate people to travel toward and with each other at work in particular ways. Among the innumerable practices that can enable or hinder high-quality connections, I will consider three: selection, socialization, and the running of meetings.

Practices of Selection
Shared values come alive when the employee selection process is geared to finding people who fit the desired culture. In creating organizations that cultivate high-quality connections, two features of selection processes are important: the means of selection and the basis of selection.

Formal Versus Informal Means of Selection. Some organizations use referrals and recommendations from current employees to attract people who fit the culture. Informal networks can be important transmitters of information about who are the good-fit candidates for jobs, especially when fit revolves around the so-called softer, more difficult to measure qualities of individuals such as respectfulness or openness that are central to building high-quality connections.[20] Charlie Alvarez, vice president of corporate development at PSS World Medical, describes the premium the firm puts on not having a negative attitude—a factor one can discern often through informal as opposed to formal recruiting channels: "We hire people like ourselves. I like to be associated with people who are ambitious, driven, competitive, athletic. I don't care how good a sales rep is, how much money he drives into the branch, if he's negative and brings the branch down."[21]

Two management experts, Charles O'Reilly and Jeff Pfeffer, report a story from Southwest Airlines that also supports this

clue. In this case, peer recruiting unearthed important information that eliminated an employee because of potential lack of fit
with Southwest's team culture: "They turned down a top pilot
who worked for another airline and did stunt work for movie
studios. Even though he was a great pilot, he made the mistake
of being rude to a Southwest receptionist."[22] In addition, the use
of peer recruiting tills the soil of connection as people have a
basis for connection before they even walk through the organization's doorway.

Relational Skills as a Basis for Selection. Organizations can choose
to emphasize or ignore relational skills in their search for and
choice of new employees. With the growing interest in emotional intelligence, more and more organizations are tuned in
to the importance of employees' "ability to process emotion-
laden information competently, and to use it to guide cognitive
activities like problem solving and to focus energy on required
behaviors."[23] As proponents of emotional intelligence in organizations suggest, effective relationship management abilities
are essential tools for building connections that enable resonance between people, facilitating motivation and collective
action when needed.[24]

Relational skills are capable of being cultivated. They are
also qualities that may be used when someone is being selected
for membership in an organization. Where skills like team building, conflict management, interpersonal development, and other
competencies that make up the relational part of emotional intelligence are considered as selection criteria, the organization is
likely to be composed of people who have the skills to foster
high-quality connections.

Evaluative tools have emerged to assess leaders' capabilities on emotional intelligence. These assessments are being used
to select and develop managers, as well as to assess how prepared a company is for future leadership demands. For example,

the ECI (Emotional Competence Inventory) is a 360-degree measure of emotional intelligence for leaders that has been used by global pharmaceutical company Johnson & Johnson to evaluate and develop its high-potential talent pool.[25]

Practices and Processes of Socialization
The socialization process describes the formal and informal means by which an organization brings a new member on board to become a part of or an insider to the system. From the moment new employees come into contact with the organization, they are exposed to messages about what is valued and devalued in terms of connection. These early messages are particularly powerful because entry into an organization is a transition point at which employees are open to learning what the organization is really like. It is also a time when current employees may be most receptive to forming connections with newcomers. In some organizations the message is communicated quickly that the organization values and enables connection, while in others the message is just the opposite.

My daughter Cara's experience when she became a new member of a local health care organization (CAMRC, or the Center for Complementary and Alternative Medicine Research Center) as a summer intern is a telling example. On her first day at work, Cara was greeted by her assigned advocate. Never having had this experience before, Cara was astonished to learn that she had been assigned an advocate to ensure that she would meet the right people, maintain access to interesting work, and have ready access to someone who could share "the way things work around here." Beyond her advocate, each person with whom she had contact encouraged her to provide input, and she was affirmed when she expressed her views. This early socialization led Cara to desire and create connections with others as she sensed they were doing toward her. What she found so surprising was the deep interest in her as an individual that people expressed and acted on. If this was the experience of an intern, destined to be there for just two months during the summer, it bodes well for the connection possibilities awaiting employees who join the organization on a more permanent basis.

Cara's experience stands in stark contrast to Ted Glittal's socialization encounter with Adeli Consulting (a fictitious name). Ted secured a summer internship at Adeli after his first year of MBA training. With six years of intense and valuable experience as a founder of a biotech start-up, Ted was a prize catch. He received several internship offers even in a tight market, but chose Adeli because of the promised chance to work in a new division devoted to strategic planning in biotech industries. After moving his family to New York for the ten-week stint (no small accomplishment), he arrived the first day to learn no one was expecting him. Although he had notified the company of his arrival date, because of a communication breakdown people were ill prepared to orient him to the firm or to his internship job. A staff member gave him materials to read, and his immediate boss took him out for lunch the first day, but Ted felt as if he was imposing on an already overburdened staff. After two weeks, Ted had met only half the people in his unit. While things improved substantially over the last eight weeks, Ted's initial experience tainted his reaction to the rest of the time spent at Adeli. He got the offer to work there permanently but turned it down. The poor connecting efforts during his initial orientation time "soured the grapes" (as he put it) and turned Ted away from Adeli as an employer and probably as a business partner as well.

These two examples highlight the vital clues about connection that relate to the way newcomers are socialized. Affirmative clues include the following:

- The organization provides multiple connecting opportunities for the new employee to meet the rest of the staff.

- The connecting opportunities are substantive and provide genuine opportunities for people to connect based on expressing and understanding real interests.
- Individuals are assigned responsibility for helping new members connect.
- People without formal responsibility for socialization willingly devote time and attention to getting a newcomer on board.
- New employees are given access to useful information that facilitates future connections (e-mail listings, FAQs about how things run, and the like).
- The process of connecting is facilitated on an ongoing and enduring basis.

Practices Used in Meetings

The ways in which meetings are designed and conducted are both indicators and creators of possibilities for high-quality connection in an organization. Most employees spend extensive time in meetings. Meetings (face-to-face, and increasingly virtual) are the sites for much of the coordination and updating work of an organization. They are where much of the contact work happens, making them important conduits and enablers of connection. Meetings can have important strategic consequences for an organization because they can spark or kill the productive conversations through which people share knowledge and build connection. As strategy experts Georg von Krogh, Kaz Ichigo, and Ikujiro Nonaka put it, "Good conversations are the cradle of social knowledge in any organization. Through extended discussions which can encompass personal flights of fancy as well as careful expositions of ideas, individual knowledge is turned into themes available for others."[26]

Three features of meetings can be potent clues for discerning whether the organization is ripe for high-quality connections. First, are meetings run so that the participants have an opportunity to quickly understand what people's various roles and agendas are for the meeting? If this knowledge is conveyed and understood, people can connect in ways that affirm their contribution and usefulness to the work of the meeting. Well-run meetings are connecting forums where work is not compromised for relationships, nor relationships for the sake of work, but rather where the two work effectively together.

Second, are meetings conducted in ways that encourage and reward people for listening to each other? Simple and obvious as this point may sound, it is stunning to reflect on how often work meetings are marked by the absence of genuine, effective listening and mutual engagement. Listening well not only facilitates connection but contributes to the efficient and effective allocation of a vital resource—time.

Third, are meetings lively and fun? The stereotypic image of meetings is that they are a time to sleep. One of my colleagues at the University of Michigan, John Tropman, has studied "meeting masters" as part of his extensive work on the conduct of meetings.[27] He finds that people who are truly expert at running meetings create occasions in which four features are present: accomplishment, limited decision rework, high-quality decisions, and fun and involvement. If meetings are run so that the structure and process create opportunities for people to engage each other in a way that is playful and enjoyable at the same time that it is productive, they can be important occasions for cultivating enlivening connections.

Clue 5: Practices and Processes for Interpersonal Helping

Organizations vary in the degree to which helping others is a normal and easy part of what people do at work. Where informal and formal systems facilitate this form of interrelation, high-quality connections are more likely to form.

Informal Norms for Helping

Informal norms for helping and teaching are important clues for discerning a high-quality context. Helping and teaching behaviors pass knowledge between people quickly. They also strengthen people's willingness to be vulnerable because they don't have to worry about always having the right answer. Interpersonal helping is essential for knowledge creation.[28]

In some organizations, asking for or needing help is the kiss of death. In others, helping is the currency through which people interrelate and do their work. Organizations can do many things to foster interpersonal helping. They can evaluate and reward helping. They can encourage the sharing of stories that make heroes out of people who save the day through helping others. Beyond affirming helping as a value, these kinds of stories also carry wisdom about how to do the relational work of helping, which improves the overall system's learning capability.

At Foote Hospital in Jackson, Michigan, my colleagues and I have studied the extraordinary accomplishments of the Physician Billing Department. It is normal and expected for individuals and groups in that department to ask for and provide help, especially in getting up to speed around new and challenging billing dilemmas. A department member describes the reality of the helping norm and its effects in these terms: "If one's group is having trouble and getting behind and just needs help for a few days, everybody pitches in . . . brings them up to par where their stress isn't too bad. . . . It makes you feel good too. Everybody here can interact with everybody's job."

Norms for helping also become apparent when members of organization are in pain of some kind. My colleagues and I have been studying compassionate responding in work organizations and have observed major differences in how and when organizations respond to members' suffering and pain. For example, we witnessed stunning contrasts in how work organizations helped or hindered employees' efforts to deal with the trauma of the September 11 tragedy at the World Trade Center. In some organizations, the entire system morphed into a healing place where leaders and processes worked together for the alleviation of suffering while trying to carry on the work of the organization.

For example, Phil Lynch, president of Reuters America, was at a board meeting of another firm when he first heard the news of the planes hitting the World Trade Center. He raced back to his office in Time Square and set up a command central on the twenty-second floor to help coordinate the efforts of all the various departments and individuals who were trying to learn of the safety of Reuters employees and customers. From the time of the initial news of the disaster until the memorial services held at the company for the two employees who died, leadership actions and processes were directed toward helping people deal with the shock and pain of the events. All communications processes were put into service for helping employees, families of employees, and customers locate loved ones. People were granted flexibility to do what they thought was necessary to expedite help to disrupted technical sites and to units who were having trouble finding employees. Psychologists were brought into the organization within twenty-four hours to help people deal with stress and uncertainty. Town hall meetings were held via teleconferencing, providing all twelve hundred employees with the chance to get updates from the leadership and to ask questions. Phil Lynch personally spent a great deal of time with the families of the employees lost in the tragedy and his personal involvement moved employees who witnessed his compassionate response. His response, in part, embodied what employees saw as the organization's response. As one employee put it, a very technical organization became flesh and blood as it transformed quickly into an organization with a heart.[29]

In other organizations, there was institutionalized denial of the people's pain and a strong push to "get back to work" and resume a "normal work pattern" as soon as possible. When norms for interpersonal helping minimized rather than magnified interpersonal helping, little healing occurred, and employee morale, engagement, and loyalty plummeted.[30]

Norms for compassionate response to the everyday pain in employees' lives are pivotal for individual and organizational outcomes. In particular, our research suggests that when people experience more compassion, they are more resourceful, cooperative, engaged, and more satisfied. They have a lower intent to leave, and they feel a stronger sense of community with the whole organization.[31] Norms for informal helping make a difference in producing this experience of compassion, and they contribute to the formation and sustenance of high-quality connections. In fact, high-quality connections beget compassion, and compassion begets more life-giving connections.

I witnessed norms for interpersonal helping unleash the healing power of interpersonal caring when one of my colleagues died while he was in Brazil teaching. Within minutes of learning of my colleague's death, the administration notified the whole community. People in a variety of roles went into action to help my colleague's family be with him in Brazil. The school planned an all-school meeting to celebrate his life. Administrators went out of their way to help and console the secretaries who had worked closely with my colleague for many years. They took the time to go for walks with people who were close to him. They contributed to a memorial on his office door that took shape during the day. Another faculty member contacted university colleagues and former students and made a book in his honor. The norm was to care and to do whatever one thought would be helpful to my colleague and to his family. There was no silencing of the pain and the emotional shock of his death. There was limited reliance on formal means to coordinate care. Rather, the norms for interpersonal helping to "do whatever fits your way of trying to help" resulted in an extraordinary response to my colleague's death.[32]

This form of improvised helping is a quality of the system that produces and is caused by high-quality connections. People acted to help because they cared for each other. Because people were so helpful and caring, the relationships between them were strengthened.

Formal Facilitation of Interpersonal Helping
When employees face trauma or unexpected illnesses, deaths in the family, and other challenges in their lives, often other employees feel called to help. Compassion and help come in all kinds of forms—money, food, physical assistance, cards, thoughtful remembrances. In most organizations, these kinds of helping efforts are improvised and newly made each time a new circumstance is faced. However, some organizations have systems in place that facilitate the coordination of care and help when employees face troubles in their lives. These kinds of programs signal a valuing of human connections by institutionalizing these values in formal programs.

At Foote Hospital in Jackson, Michigan, employees wanted to help a colleague who had lost three close relatives, so they lobbied for a system whereby they could donate vacation and personal time to others. This initiative is now formalized as a program that allows people to give time away to other employees. VeriFone has a program like this as well, called VeriGift. The program was officially made policy after employees spontaneously created a pool of vacation time to help a salesman whose wife was terminally ill.[33]

Cisco Systems has a similar philosophy, although it has created a different set of programs. Rather than having people donate time to each other, Cisco uses its coordinating muscle to facilitate unit efforts to coordinate money and other resources being offered to fellow employees. Managers in Human Resources see the use of the organization's coordination resources to facilitate employees' helping each other as an investment in the quality of connection between people. In organizations that have these kinds of programs, healthy connections are more likely to thrive.

Clue 6: Design of Physical Space

Physical design is one of the "levers you can pull to manage the conditions of interaction in an organization."[34] Physical space reveals much about how likely people are to be connected, and maybe even about the quality of that connection.

Does the physical space invite connection? For example, does the physical space convey an openness that motivates and facilitates connecting behaviors? The designer of the Cornelia Street and River Café in Greenwich Village has a green courtyard at the café's entrance. The building's architect, Richard Rogers, describes the effect of this physical space feature: "It gives that essential feeling of openness, and it is a place where people gather and meet, where unexpected things happen."[35]

In the new Reuters America building at 3 Times Square, the heart of the business involves securing and distributing financial news. In the design of the new building, special attention was paid to creating open spaces and low physical barriers between employees to encourage collaboration and quick information transfer, and to minimize status differences that might get in the way of rapid response and flexible information sharing.

Does the physical space create strong or weak status differences between people? Power differences interfere with the connecting process.[36] If people are separated not only by physical partitions and space but by symbolic displays—uniforms, office size and location, type and quality of furniture—that communicate messages of distinctions in status and power, it may become more challenging to build connections between people. In fact, it was the belief that power differences make it more difficult for people to connect that helped to usher in the trend toward casual dress Fridays in many U.S. firms. It was thought that the symbol of casual dress made it easier for people to build connections with each other as one formal reminder of hierarchy and status differences was removed, at least for a day.

Clue 7: Leadership Qualities and Behaviors

The clues discussed to this point (values, rewards, structure) are often direct reflections of past and current leadership actions. Thus some of the leadership behaviors that are likely to contribute to creating and sustaining high-quality connections are implicit in the discussion so far. Here I turn to more personal actions that signal leaders' commitment to fostering these kinds of connections.

A leader's every move affirms or disconfirms the potential for building high-quality connections. Sometimes leaders are very explicit about how they see their role in this regard. Their language and their actions convey the centrality of the quality of relationships to their own sense of what leadership can accomplish. In particular, they convey their commitment in four main ways: by being vulnerable and personally open, by being relationally attentive, by choosing language and stories that celebrate and foster connection, and by creating positive images of the future.

A Leader Who Is Vulnerable and Personally Open
We look to leaders for signals about what is normal and acceptable behavior in our work organizations. As I have already discussed, being vulnerable and open creates conditions that foster mutuality and trust. If leaders can be vulnerable and open, employees feel safer and more motivated to reciprocate. When he

was CEO of Medtronic, Bill George had a personal goal of responding by the end of the day to any of the firm's seventeen thousand employees who contacted him by e-mail. He also used the e-mail system to share something of himself. During a speech in August 2001, he told of his decision to share a pre-Thanksgiving message with all his employees about the gratefulness he felt that his wife had survived a year of grueling chemotherapy for treatment of breast cancer. As he put it, "I was amazed that by expressing some vulnerability, that so many people, even three or four years later would share stories of their own—about their father, their son, themselves, their spouse." His sense was that his own willingness to be vulnerable and the company's constant communication and openness with employees contributed to people's trust in the company and in each other.

When Dick Knowles of DuPont took over the management of the company's Belle plant, he faced a difficult situation. The plant had an abysmal safety record, environmental emissions were unacceptable, relations between the plant and the local community were sour, and productivity and earnings were less than satisfactory. Knowles had made his reputation on being a cool, calm, and very controlling manager. Yet over a period of nine years, as he explains it, both he and the plant were transformed.[37] A big part of the transformation was fueled by Knowles's gradual awareness that he had to become more open and vulnerable. This meant listening to lots of bad news and not getting defensive. It meant admitting he was wrong and being emotionally vulnerable. Knowles marks his own transformation in his description of one incident in which he was receptive and open to learning what the plant's managers really thought of his leadership. His lead-in during the meeting was an admission of how he was contributing to the problem.

> So I went to the team and said, "Maybe what I'm doing is disenabling you folks. Would you be willing to talk to me about

that?" All but one of them spent about an hour telling me how great it was when I wasn't there, and what a jerk I was. They said I'd jump on them, wouldn't let them finish sentences, that I'd be really hard on someone if I thought they had done something wrong. It wasn't fun to have to sit there and listen to all this stuff, I can tell you. There was a lot of pain in me, and I cried a bit after that.[38]

A leader's willingness to be vulnerable and emotionally accessible creates a healthy basis for authentic connecting, building a foundation for high-quality relationships. And as the example of Dick Knowles suggests, where these relationships happen, communication improves, problem-solving energy is released, and the firm as well as the employees benefit.

A Leader Who Is Relationally Attentive

High-quality connections are more likely to thrive in contexts where leaders have a sensitive "relational test-kit" to know when the soil for connection is getting toxic or when it needs more fertilizing.

Relational attentiveness is a key part of emotional intelligence and is related to people's ability to perceive and respond to others' emotional state.[39] This quality stems from a genuine and deep interest in people. Hatim Tyabji, former CEO of VeriFone, described relationally attentive leaders as "being sensitive to the people in the organization" and realizing "that's what really makes the organization tick."[40] Leaders who are relationally attentive feel changes in relational dynamics and notice the emotional changes in others. Peter Frost argues that attentiveness is particularly important when leaders create pain, because they can inflict substantial damage on the connective tissue of an organization by not seeing the effects or their own or of others' wounding behaviors.[41] This was part of Bob Knowles's realization in the example of the DuPont Belle plant. The same lesson is evident in a riveting example that Frost tells of a manager who under severe deadline pressure became very curt with a team member during a meeting, silencing him and likely making others wary about participating. In the middle of the night this manager awoke, literally and figuratively, to a realization of the damage he had done. The next day, in a follow-up meeting, he publicly apologized to his victim. His apology was appreciatively accepted. Without having a relational test-kit and being attentive to his own damaging effects, this leader could have torn the connective tissue of the group, making it difficult for others to connect with him and with each other. Instead, his attentiveness led to relational repair work, and a strengthening of the connective tissue of the whole.

Relational attentiveness is also evident when leaders sense and magnify the joy, excitement, and awe associated with accomplishments, transitions, major life events, and sometimes just the daily pleasures and thrills of work life. Sarah Boidt, manager of the Billing Department at Foote Hospital, believes in marking and celebrating her team members' accomplishments and milestones. She also believes in doing whatever it takes to inject excitement into the group if spirits or energy sag. For example, she watches for signs of energy depletion and instigates play to breathe life back into the group. These interventions may involve initiating squirt gun fights or announcing what the department calls sunshine breaks, where people spill outdoors, breathe in fresh air and get reinvigorated for a ten-minute stint. A leader with this kind of relational attentiveness can play a key role in sustaining and repairing the connective tissue of a workgroup, department, or organization.

A Leader's Language and Stories
Beyond actions, one of a leader's most powerful tools is the use of words. Language, metaphors, and images can till the soil from which relationships grow and take sustenance.

A good example of a leader's use of everyday language to bridge differences and build connection is provided by Jane Pratt, former CEO of the Mountain Institute.[42] The Mountain Institute is what is called a global change organization. It is a non-profit organization designed to advance mountain cultures and preserve mountain environments all over the world. It does its work through community-based conservation and development programs that are designed to empower local groups living in the mountains as well as by facilitating global initiatives that are designed to enhance the well-being of people who live in these regions of the world. Pratt, who led the organization for eight years, was very mindful of how she used language to facilitate meaningful connections across the diverse set of partners served by the Institute. Because she convened and communicated with people from all over the world who were part of her organization, and these people came from some of the poorest of the world's regions, she was very cognizant of how technical and scientific language could make people feel stupid, causing them to censor themselves and hold back input. Consequently, she relied extensively on storytelling and simple images, purposely avoiding complex language that might make people feel incompetent or unknowing. She consciously used the language of dance and music, which she believed minimized power and status distances, and invited people to connect on the basis of heart as well as mind. Instead of using the language of conflict and interests, she talked in terms of rhythms, harmonies, and making music. Using language that tapped into the universal cultural interest in music and dance, she believed, invited people to reach out and try to connect with one another.

The role of language in facilitating high-quality connections is especially apparent when very different people are coming together to accomplish some joint task. Julia Wondolleck and Steven Yaffee have spent ten years studying the work of collaborations that bring together government agencies, communities, and private groups to work on the vexing and challenging problems of the natural environment.[43] They find that in this very contested domain of interorganizational problem solving, language use is one of the keystones for successful collaboration.

For example, Wondolleck and Yaffee tell the story of a rural community in Oregon that had long been a battleground between environmentalists concerned about endangered species, farmers and ranchers trying to maintain their livelihood, and federal public land agencies caught in the middle and demonized by both sides. Those involved readily called themselves "arch enemies" and expected to meet only across a courtroom. A gradual transformation in the language they used in reference to each other, however, introduced a dramatically changed perspective on the issues and what should be done about them. As one environmentalist recalled, they moved away from the frustrating language of "my opinion against yours; my expert against yours; my laws against your guidelines" to an inclusive view that they all shared responsibility for resolving what were, in fact, shared problems. A fifth-generation farmer embroiled in the conflict captured the transformation when saying, "In the past it has been 'us' and 'them' and now it is 'we'—it is all of us together."

High-quality connections between disparate parties in these collaborations are more likely to thrive when leaders use inclusive language that calls forth a common identity for all participants. It is language that sews people together by articulating joint ownership and positive characterizations of what each person offers to the whole. They argue that the use of language that is consistent with what they call relational thinking creates fertile ground for seeding high-quality connections.

A Leader's Positive Image of the Future

Leaders who create positive images of what an organization does and where it can go infuse energy and life into the whole.[44] They do this through three means.

First, positive images of the organization help people create positive expectations of what other organizational members offer to the whole. These expectations start to become a reality, unleashing affirming actions taken toward each other. For example, if I am an employee of *National Geographic Magazine* and find myself part of a company vision that embodies a positive image of "Celebrating What Is Right with the World," this image is likely to change how I see my work and my relationship to others.[45] Rather than being simply photographers who happen to work for a prestigious publication, we are active participants in creating a vision of what is possible. I start acting toward my colleagues as co-creators of this positive image. Because I believe the vision is worthy, I act in a more affirming way to my fellow employees.

Second, positive images of the organization unleash positive emotions that make us less self-focused, more focused on the good in the world. These emotions strengthen a sense of solidarity.[46] As I have noted several times in this book, positive emotions create powerful effects on human functioning that make us actually drawn to and more capable of being in high-quality connections. Using the example of being a *National Geographic* employee I feel joy and pride about being part of this positive image, and my emotional response makes me less self-interested and more tuned in to the needs, concerns, and actions of others.

Third, a positive image unleashes hope. Hope, in turn, creates a sense of energy and connection to others as hope helps people to feel taken care of at the same time that it helps them see a way to make a difference or to have a desired impact.[47]

Here's a different example in a very different setting to show how positive images can transform possibilities for connection. Irwin Redlener is a physician who created an image that has become reality at Montefiore Medical Center in the Bronx.[48] Dr. Redlener envisions a hospital as a "medical home" for every child who lacks continuous access to high-quality, comprehensive health care. He has the compelling positive image of a hospital as a place that changes kids' lives. It does this by "providing excellent health care and a total environment that ignites the imagination of children." For example, each room at the hospital has an interactive virtual portal that connects the child and the child's family to a world of discovery, opening up new worlds that kids can explore. The inspiration for this idea is captured in the questions the designer, Jeb Weisman, posed: "Wouldn't it be great if you could learn something about poetry, painting, chemistry, space or oceanography while you were here?" In addition, each floor of the hospital is designed to represent a different part of the cosmos. An interactive playground on each floor is designed to encourage children to engage this part of the cosmos. Even the window shades are custom-made murals that fit the theme of the floor. There are no patient room numbers, only room designations that fit some exploratory theme, such as the Big Dipper Room. In such a world, "children are explorers on a journey to health." To make the image a reality has required rethinking the nature of hospitals, the role of doctors, and the standard approach to pediatric health care. The whole organization has worked to physically create a hospital that is "as much about discovery as recovery." The positive image of what the organization could be and is creates fertile ground for meaningful connection between employees who share the vision, and with hospital patients and families who live this image as customers in a really different health care system.

■ Putting the Clues to Work: Strengthening
   the Connective Tissue in Your Organization

Clearly there are many indicators to look for when trying to
crack the code that governs whether an organizational context
is one in which high-quality connections flourish. Exhibit 6.1
summarizes the clue set discussed in this chapter. Your task as
a manager is to use these clues to diagnose your own organization and do what you can to help make your own work unit and
organization a fertile environment for life-giving connections.

As a manager, you can have significant influence in your
immediate environment simply by making the quality of connections a priority and using the strategies in this book to set an
example for others and to coach those you manage. Creating
large-scale organizational change, of course, is a different and
momentous challenge. Meaningful change in any of the domains
of organizational life discussed in this chapter often requires
deep change, the kind of change that penetrates to the core of individuals and organizations.[49] Although it is beyond the scope
of this book to develop how such change can be brought about,
I can provide a few guidelines that would be useful to keep in
mind as you think about your role as a change agent.

First, communicate continuously in clear and compelling
ways why change is necessary. Know and articulate the value
of high-quality connections to the strategic goals of the organization and the cost of neglecting this key dimension of organizational life.

Second, engage in genuine dialogue with subordinates,
peers, and upper management about how change directed toward building a work unit or organization based on high-quality connections will be accomplished. Make sure those affected
by the change have input into what will be done and how. Engaging others honors the values necessary to foster the context

Exhibit 6.1. **Cracking the Code: Clues for Assessing Whether Your Organization Is Fertile Ground for Growing High-Quality Connections**

In the column at the right, indicate your assessment of how strong your organization or work unit is with respect to each clue. You can use this "report card" to assess the current conditions in your organization and target areas you would like to work on changing. You can then use the report card to re-assess any of these areas to measure progress.

Values • Valuing teams and teamwork • Valuing the development of people • Valuing of the whole person • Valuing of respect and dignity	
Formal and Informal Rewards and Recognition • Rewards given for collective performance • Rewards given for enabling others • Frequent formal and informal recognition of contributions	
Structure, the Division of Labor, and the Power of Networks • Limited vertical layers and hierarchy • Active networks and multiple ties between people	

Exhibit 6.1. Cracking the Code: Clues for Assessing Whether Your Organization Is Fertile Ground for Growing High-Quality Connections, Cont'd

Practices and Processes for Getting Things Done ■ Selection practices that involve employees and include relational skills as a basis of selection ■ Socialization practices that provide multiple, substantive connecting opportunities ■ Meeting practices that encourage connection	
Practices and Processes for Interpersonal Helping ■ Informal and formal norms for helping ■ Formal facilitation of helping	
Design of Physical Space ■ Open space that minimizes status and power differences and invites connection	
Qualities and Behaviors of Leaders ■ Being vulnerable and open ■ Being relationally attentive ■ Using language and stories that celebrate and support connection ■ Creating a positive image of the future	

for high-quality connections and ensures that you will get vital information and feedback about what will work and what will not. In short, make the change process itself an occasion for working toward building high-quality connections by engaging the people who will be affected in a way that is respectful, builds trust, and is task enabling.

Third, start small. Use management scholar Karl Weick's compelling "small wins" strategy to build positive momentum and a sense of efficacy and success that helps to keep the change moving.[50] A small win might be successful advocacy of a change in recognition and reward systems that brings visibility to the enabling that people in your organization are doing for each other. A more informal small win might be simply creating more ways of talking about the contributions that people make to each other's work or an opportunity to discuss how vital trust is in producing results in your unit. Small wins add up. They begin the process of transformation. They endow people with a sense that change is possible and yields results, which invites more change.

Fourth, be patient and persistent. Remember that all organizations pose many challenges to meaningful change. It's normal to feel discouraged at times about whether change is really happening or is yielding the intended results. It will help if you have a reasonable time line and remain flexible so that you can improvise and try new avenues if current efforts are thwarted. And, of course, if your best efforts aren't enough, you now have all the clues you need to find an organization that is more congenial to the high-quality connections that can enable you to thrive in your chosen profession.

■ A Closing Word

In this book, I have discussed the sources, nature, and results of high-quality connections on both the micro level of everyday interactions and the macro level of organizational conditions that foster this kind of productive, energizing relationship. My hope is that the book charges you up to become a manager of high-quality connections. With this charge, you become the architect of contexts at work that enable life-giving connections between people. With this charge, you also attend to your own and others' everyday interactions, to assess and facilitate interaction pathways that build and sustain rather than diminish and destroy this vital form of connecting. Finally, with this charge you are equipped to notice and begin to work to help people with corrosive connections, knowing full well the lasting damage they do to the individuals involved and to the organization as a whole. I have faith that by taking the building and sustaining of high-quality connections seriously as a strategic objective to pursue every day, you will be progressing down the path of becoming extraordinary both as an individual manager and as an organizational leader.

CHAPTER SUMMARY

This chapter identified seven major clues that signal an organizational context in which high-quality connections thrive:

1. Values, in particular the valuing of teams, the development of people, respect, and dignity
2. The design of informal and formal reward systems to align them with collective performance, enablement, and contributing to others
3. An organizational structure and division of labor that minimizes vertical distance and hierarchy while cultivating the power of networks and multiple ties between people
4. Practices and processes for getting things done, selecting and socializing employees, and conducting meetings
5. Practices and processes that encourage interpersonal helping
6. The design of physical surroundings
7. Leadership qualities and behavior, including being vulnerable and open, being relationally attentive, using language that is inclusive and rich, and affirming positive images

As a manager, you can use these clues to diagnose how well your organization and work unit currently support the growth of high-quality connections and to set goals for change efforts. Here are four guidelines to keep in mind as you work for positive change:

- Continually communicate the need for change in compelling ways that relate the benefits to the organization's strategic goals.
- Actively engage those who will be affected by the change.
- Strive for small wins.
- Be patient and persistent.

Notes

Chapter One

1. Jane E. Dutton and Emily Heaphy, "The Power of High Quality Connections," in *Positive Organizational Scholarship,* edited by Kim Cameron, Jane Dutton, and Robert Quinn (San Francisco: Berrett-Koehler, 2003).

2. Peter J. Frost, *Toxic Emotions at Work* (Boston: Harvard Business School Press, 2003).

3. Energy is an affective experience defined by some researchers as *energetic arousal* (see Robert. E. Thayer, *The Biopsychology of Mood and Arousal* (New York: Oxford University Press, 1989); *subjective energy* (see S. R. Marks, "Multiple Roles and Role Strain: Some Notes of Human Energy, Time and Commitment," *American Sociological Review* 42, no. 6 (1977): 921–936); or *emotional energy* (see Randall Collins, "On the Micro Foundation of Macro-Sociology," *American Journal of Sociology* 6 (1981): 984–1014).

4. Jean Baker Miller and Irene P. Stiver, *The Healing Connection* (Boston: Beacon Press, 1997).

5. From interview with William Robertson, CEO of Weston Solutions, February 22, 2002.

6. Barbara L. Fredrickson, "Positive Emotions," in *Handbook of Positive Psychology,* edited by C. R. Snyder and Shane J. Lopez (New York: Oxford University Press, 2002), pp. 120–134.

7. Robert Cross, Wayne Baker, and Andrew Parker, "Charged Up: The Creation and Depletion of Energy in Social Networks," Working paper, University of Virginia McIntyre School of Commerce, 2003, p. 17. (This paper is scheduled for publication in *Sloan Management Review,* probably in late 2003.) See also Wayne Baker, Rob Cross, and Melissa Wooten, "Positive Organizational Network Analysis and Energizing Relationships," in *Positive Organizational Scholarship,* edited by Cameron, Dutton, and Quinn.

8. Lynn M. Andersson and Christine M. Pearson, "Tit for Tat? The Spiraling Effect of Incivility in the Workplace," *Academy of Management Review* 24 (1999): 452–471.

9. Christine M. Pearson, Lynn M. Andersson, and Christine L. Porath, "Assessing and Attacking Workplace Incivility," *Organizational Dynamics* (Fall 2000): 123–137.

10. Karen S. Rook, "Negative Social Interactions: Impact on Psychological Well-Being," *Journal of Personality and Social Psychology* 46, no. 5 (1984): 1097–1108.

11. Bennet J. Tepper, "Consequences of Abusive Supervision," *Academy of Management Journal* 43 (2000): 178–190. See p. 178.

12. Blake Ashforth, "Petty Tyranny in Organizations: A Preliminary Examination of Antecedents and Consequences," *Canadian Journal of Administrative Sciences* 14 (1998): 755–778.

13. Tepper, "Consequences of Abusive Supervision."

14. Sandra L. Robinson and Anne M. O'Leary-Kelly, "Monkey See, Monkey Do: The Influence of Work Groups on the Antisocial Behavior of Employees," *Academy of Management Journal* 41, no. 6 (1998): 658–672.

15. Frost uses the same example from this conversation in *Toxic Emotions at Work,* p. 92.

16. For two excellent summaries of the impact of positive relationships in life more generally, see Harry Reis and Shelly L. Gable, "Toward a Positive Psychology of Relationships," in *Flourishing: Positive Psychology and the Life Well-Lived,* edited by Corey L. M. Keyes and

Jonathan Haidt (Washington, DC: American Psychological Association, 2003), pp. 129–160; and Ellen Bersheid, "The Human's Greatest Strength: Other Humans," in *A Psychology of Human Strengths,* edited by Lisa G. Aspinwall and Ursula M. Staudinger (Washington, DC: American Psychological Association, 2003), pp. 37–48.

17. A helpful edited volume that documents a range of these effects is Carol D. Ryff and Burton H. Singer (eds.), *Emotion, Social Relationships and Health* (New York: Oxford University Press, 2001).

18. Harry T. Reiss, Kenneth M. Sheldon, Shelly L. Gable, J. Roscoe, and Micheal Ryan. "Daily Well-Being: The Role of Autonomy, Competence and Relatedness," *Personality and Social Psychological Bulletin* 26 (2000): 419–435.

19. Re longer life, see James. S. House, K. R. Landis, and D. Umberson, "Social Relationships and Health," *Science* 241 (1988): 540–545. Re reduced risk of death, see Teresa F. Seeman, "Social Ties and Health: The Benefits of Social integration," *Annals of Epidemiology* 6 (1996): 442–451. Re health benefits, see B. N. Uchino, J. T. Cacioppo, and J. K. Kiecolt-Glaser, "The Relationship between Social Support and Physiological Processes: A Review with Emphasis on Underlying Mechanisms and Implications for Health," *Psychological Bulletin* 119, no. 3 (1996): 488–531. Re reduced stress, see Peggy Thoits, "Stress, Coping and Social Support Processes: Where Are We? What Next?" *Journal of Health and Social Behavior* 35 (1995): 53–79. For review of some of these effects and others see Teresa Seeman, "How Do Others Get Under Our Skin? Social Relationships and Health," in *Emotion, Social Relationships and Health,* edited by Carol D. Ryff and Burton H. Singer (New York; Oxford University Press, 2001), pp. 189–210.

20. Michele Williams and Jane E. Dutton, "Corrosive Political Climates: The Heavy Toll of Negative Political Behavior in Organizations," in *The Pressing Problems of Modern Organizations: Transforming the Agenda for Research and Practice,* edited by Robert E. Quinn, Regina M. O'Neill, and Linda St. Clair (New York: American Management Association, 1999), pp. 3–30.

21. William Kahn, "Relational Systems at Work," in *Research in Organizational Behavior,* Vol. 20, edited by Barry M. Staw and Larry L. Cummings (Greenwich, CT: JAI Press, 1998), pp. 39–76.

22. Roger Lewin and Birute Regine, *The Soul at Work* (New York: Simon & Schuster, 2000), p. 294.

23. Wayne Baker, *Achieving Success Through Social Capital* (San Francisco: Jossey-Bass, 2000).

24. Barbara L. Fredrickson, "What Good Are Positive Emotions?" *Review of General Psychology* 2, no. 3 (1998): 300–319.

25. Fredrickson, "What Good Are Positive Emotions?"

26. Julian E. Orr, *Talking About Machines* (Ithaca, NY: Cornell University Press, 1996).

27. Jody Hoffer Gittell, *The Southwest Airlines Way: Using the Power of Relationships to Achieve High Performance* (New York: McGraw-Hill, 2003).

28. Jody Hoffer Gittell, "A Relational Theory of Coordination," in *Positive Organizational Scholarship,* edited by Cameron, Dutton, and Quinn.

29. Guiseppe Labianca, E. Umphress, and J. Kaufmann, "A Preliminary Test of the Negative Asymmetry Hypothesis in Workplace Social Networks," paper presented at the National Academy of Management meetings, Toronto, August 2000.

30. David S. Pottruck and Terry Pearce, *Clicks and Mortar: Passion Driven Growth in an Internet Driven World* (San Francisco: Jossey-Bass, 2000).

31. Bruce Kogut and U. Zander, "Knowledge of the Firm, Combinative Capabilities and Replication of Technology," *Organizational Science* 3, no. 3 (1992): 383–397.

32. D. L. Rulke, S. Zaheer, and M. H. Anderson, "Sources of Managers' Knowledge of Organizational Capabilities," *Organizational Behavior and Human Decision Processes* 82, no. 1 (2000): 134–149.

33. Jean Lave and Etienne Wenger, *Situated Learning: Legitimate Peripheral Participation* (New York: Cambridge University Press, 1991).

34. Lewin and Regine, *The Soul at Work.*

35. Lewin and Regine, *The Soul at Work,* p. 26.

Chapter Two

1. For recent evidence see L. M. Cortina, V. J. Magley, J. H. Williams, and R. D. Langhout, "Incivility in the Workplace: Incidence and Impact," *Journal of Occupational Health Psychology* 6 (2000): 64–80;

or Christine M. Pearson, Lynn A. Andersson, and Christine L. Porath, "Assessing and Attacking Workplace Incivility," *Organizational Dynamics* (2000): 123–137.

2. Pearson, Andersson, and Porath, "Assessing and Attacking Workplace Incivility," p. 123.

3. Susan Shellenbarger, "From Our Readers: The Bosses That Drove Me to Quit My Job," *Wall Street Journal* (February 9, 2000): B1.

4. Joshua D. Margolis, "Responsibility in Organizational Context," *Business Ethics Quarterly* 11 (2001): 431–454.

5. Jean Baker Miller and Irene P. Stiver, *The Healing Connection* (Boston: Beacon Press, 1997).

6. Marshall B. Rosenberg, *Nonviolent Communication* (Encinatas, CA: PuddleDancer Press, 2000), p. 98.

7. Edward M. Hallowell, *Connect: Twelve Vital Ties That Open Your Heart, Lengthen Your Life and Deepen Your Soul* (New York: Pantheon Books, 1999), p. 126.

8. Joost A. Meerloo, "Conversation and Communication," in *The Human Dialogue,* edited by F. W. Matson and A. Montagu (New York: Free Press, 1967), p. 147.

9. Albert Mehrabian as cited in Matthew McKay, Martha Davis, and Patrick Fanning, *Messages: The Communication Skills Book* (Oakland, CA: New Harbinger, 1995), p. 53.

10. Vanessa Williams and Richard Williams, *Lifeskills* (New York: Random House, 1997), p. 85.

11. Susan Harter, "Authenticity," in *Handbook of Positive Psychology,* edited by C. R. Snyder and S. J. Lopez (New York: Oxford University Press, 2002), pp. 382 394.

12. Rachel N. Remen, *My Grandfather's Blessings* (New York: Rivethead Press, 2000), p. 5.

13. Rosamund Stone Zander and Benjamin Zander, *The Art of Possibility: Transforming Professional and Personal Life* (Boston: Harvard Business School Press, 2000), p. 26.

14. Deborah M. Kolb and Judith Williams, *The Shadow Negotiation* (New York: Simon & Schuster, 2000), p. 140.

15. Kolb and Williams, *The Shadow Negotiation,* p. 159.

16. Charles A. O'Reilly and Jeffrey Pfeffer, *Hidden Value* (Cambridge, MA: Harvard University Press, 2000), p. 74.

17. Kepner-Tregoe, "People and Their Jobs: What's Real, What's Rhetoric?" (cited in James M. Kouzes and Barry Z. Posner, *Encouraging the Heart: A Leader's Guide to Rewarding and Recognizing Others* (San Francisco: Jossey-Bass, 1999), p. 4).

18. Judith B. Jordan, "The Meaning of Mutuality," in *Women's Growth in Connection,* edited by Judith V. Jordon, Alexandra G. Kaplan, Jean Baker Miller, Irene P. Stiver, and Janet L. Surrey (New York: Guilford Press 1991), p. 82.

19. John Kelly and David Stark, "Crisis, Recovery, Innovation: Learning from 9/11," *Environmental and Planning A* 34 (2002): 1523–1533.

20. Roger Lewin and Birute Regine, *The Soul at Work* (New York: Simon & Schuster, 2000), p. 312.

21. Lewin and Regine, *The Soul at Work,* p. 130.

22. Max Messmer, "Improving Your Listening Skills," *Management Accounting* 79, no. 9 (1998): 14–18.

23. Michele Williams, "Seeing Through the Client's Eyes: Building Interpersonal Trust, Cooperation, and Performance Across Organizational Boundaries," unpublished doctoral dissertation, University of Michigan, 2001.

24. Lucy Candib, *Medicine and the Family* (New York: Basic Books, 1995).

25. McKay, Davis, and Fanning, *Messages.*

26. Rosenberg, *Nonviolent Communication.*

27. Rosenberg, *Nonviolent Communication,* p. 89.

28. Marshall Rosenberg, keynote presentation at the NCME National Conference (1999), as cited in Rosenberg, *Nonviolent Communication,* p. 83.

29. David A. Whetten and Kim S. Cameron, *Developing Management Skills,* 4th ed. (Reading, MA: Addison-Wesley, 1999).

30. Whetten and Cameron, *Developing Management Skills,* pp. 202–203.

31. Whetten and Cameron, *Developing Management Skills,* p. 203.

32. Susan Fiske and E. Depret, "Control, Interdependence and Power: Understanding Social Cognition in Its Social Context," in *European Review of Social Psychology,* Vol. 7, edited by W. Stroebe and W. Hewtone (New York: Wiley, 1996), pp. 31–61.

Chapter Three

1. Phil Jackson, Hugh Delehanty, and Bill Bradley, *Sacred Hoops: Spiritual Lessons of a Hardwood Warrior* (New York: Hyperion Books, 1997), p. 152.
2. Leslie A. Perlow, *Finding Time: How Corporations, Individuals, and Families Can Benefit from New Work Practices* (Cambridge, MA: MIT Press, 1997), p. 66.
3. Jody H. Gittell, "Paradox of Coordination and Control," *California Management Review* 42 (2000): 10.
4. Ram Dass and Paul Gorman, *How Can I Help? Stories and Reflections on Service* (New York: Knopf, 1985).
5. Joyce K. Fletcher, *Disappearing Acts: Gender, Power and Relational Practice at Work* (Cambridge, MA: MIT Press, 1999), p. 58.
6. I have benefited greatly in this categorization scheme from the work of Regina O'Neill, who did a comprehensive review of mentoring and social support literature and shared with me her working paper titled "Helping Behaviors: An Integrative Approach to Mentoring and Social Support."
7. Judith V. Jordan, "The Meaning of Mutuality," in *Women's Growth in Connection,* edited by Judith V. Jordon, Alexandra G. Kaplan, Jean Baker Miller, Irene P. Stiver, and Janet L. Surrey (New York: Guilford Press, 1991).
8. Jennifer Reingold, "Teacher in Chief," *Fast Company* (September 2001): 64.
9. There are lots of terrific studies of the effects of mentoring on career outcomes. See Belle Rose Ragins and John L. Cotton, "Mentor Functions and Outcomes: A Comparison of Men and Women in Formal and Informal Mentoring Relationships," *Journal of Applied Psychology* 84 (1999): 529–550, as one example.
10. Fletcher, *Disappearing Acts,* p. 56.
11. K. E. Weick, "Small Wins: Redefining the Scale of Social Problems," *American Psychologist* 39 (1984): 40–49.
12. Richard W. Griffin, "Objective and Social Sources of Information in Task Redesign: A Field Experiment," *Administrative Science Quarterly* 28 (1983): 184–200.

13. Max DePree, *Leadership Is an Art* (New York: Doubleday/Currency, 1989).

14. Rosabeth Moss Kanter, *Men and Women of the Corporation* (New York: Basic Books, 1977).

15. See, for example, Wayne Baker, *Achieving Success Through Social Capital* (San Francisco: Jossey-Bass, 2000), or Ronald S. Burt, *Structural Holes: The Social Structure of Competition* (Cambridge, MA: Harvard University Press, 1992).

16. Connie Gersick, Jean Bartunek, and Jane E. Dutton, "Learning From Academia: The Importance of Relationships in Professional Life," *Academy of Management Journal* 43 (2000): 1026–1044. The names are fictitious to preserve anonymity in the quote.

17. Kanter, *Men and Women of the Corporation.*

18. K. E. Kram, *Mentoring at Work: Developmental Relationships in Organizational Life* (Glenview, IL: Scott Foresman, 1985) p. 30.

19. Fletcher, *Disappearing Acts.*

20. Michele Williams and Jane E. Dutton, "Corrosive Political Climates: The Heavy Toll of Negative Political Behavior in Organizations," in *The Pressing Problems of Modern Organizations: Transforming the Agenda for Research and Practice,* edited by R. E. Quinn, R. M. O'Neill, and L. St. Clair (New York: American Management Association), pp. 3–30.

21. Kram, *Mentoring at Work,* p. 33.

22. Kram, *Mentoring at Work,* p. 34.

23. William A. Kahn, "Secure Base Relationships at Work," in *The Career Is Dead—Long Live the Career: A Relational Approach to Careers,* edited by Douglas T. Hall and Associates (San Francisco: Jossey-Bass, 1996), pp. 158–179.

24. Kram, *Mentoring at Work,* p. 37.

25. James M. Kouzes and Barry Z. Posner, *Encouraging the Heart: A Leader's Guide to Rewarding and Recognizing Others* (San Francisco: Jossey-Bass, 1999), p. 7.

26. Fiona Lee, "When the Going Gets Tough, Do the Tough Ask for Help? Help Seeking and Power Motivation in Organizations," *Organizational Behavior and Human Decision Processes* 7 (1997): 336–363.

27. David Thomas, "Racial Dynamics in Cross-Race Developmental Relationships," *Administrative Science Quarterly* 38 (1993): 188.

28. Fletcher, *Disappearing Acts.*
29. Fletcher, *Disappearing Acts,* p. 95.

Chapter Four

1. J. G. Holmes and J. K. Rempel, "Trust in Close Relationships," in *Review of Personality and Social Psychology,* Vol. 10, edited by C. Hendrick (Thousand Oaks, CA: Sage, 1989), pp. 187–219; and R. C. Mayer and J. H. Davis, "The Effect of the Performance Appraisal System on Trust for Management: A Field Quasi-Experiment," *Journal of Applied Psychology* 84 (1999): 123–136.
2. Roy J. Lewicki and Barbara Benedict Bunker, "Developing and Maintaining Trust in Work Relationships," in *Trust in Organizations,* edited by R. M. Kramer and T. R. Tyler (Thousand Oaks, CA: Sage Publications, 1996), pp. 114–139.
3. Ann Marie Zak, Joel A. Gold, Richard Ryckman, and Ellen Lenney, "Assessments of Trust in Intimate Relationships and the Self-Perception Process," *Journal of Social Psychology* 138, no. 2 (1998): 217–228.
4. Michele Williams, "In Whom We Trust: Group Membership as an Affective Context for Trust Development," *Academy of Management Review* 26, no. 3 (2001): 377–396.
5. Dale E. Zand, "Trust and Managerial Problem Solving," *Administrative Science Quarterly* 17, no. 2 (1972): 229–239.
6. Dale E. Zand, *The Leadership Triad: Knowledge, Trust and Power* (New York: Oxford University Press, 1997), p. 92.
7. N. L. Rackham, L. Friedman, and R. Ruff, *Getting Partnering Right* (New York: McGraw-Hill, 1996).
8. Deborah M. Kolb and Judith Williams, *The Shadow Negotiation* (New York: Simon & Schuster, 2000), p. 249.
9. James M. Kouzes and Barry Z. Posner, *The Leadership Challenge* (San Francisco: Jossey-Bass, 1995), p. 167.
10. Roger Lewin and Birute Regine, *The Soul at Work* (New York: Simon & Schuster, 2000), p. 132.
11. Lewin and Regine, *The Soul at Work,* p. 132.
12. Lewin and Regine, *The Soul at Work,* p. 305.

13. Dennis S. Reina and Michelle L. Reina, *Trust and Betrayal in the Workplace* (San Francisco: Berrett-Koehler, 1999), p. 103.
14. Rackham, Friedman, and Ruff, *Getting Partnering Right.* Story of Cyndie is on p. 85.
15. Zand, *The Leadership Triad,* p. 92.
16. Lewin and Regine, *The Soul at Work,* p. 9.
17. Brian Uzzi, "Social Structure and Competition in Interfirm Networks: The Paradox of Embeddedness," *Administrative Science Quarterly* 42 (1997): 335–367.
18. Peter J. Frost, *Toxic Emotions at Work* (Boston: Harvard Business School Press, 2003).
19. Lewicki and Bunker, "Developing and Maintaining Trust in Work Relationships," p. 127.
20. Lewin and Regine, *The Soul at Work,* p. 162.
21. David H. Maister, Charles H. Green, and Robert M. Galford, *The Trusted Advisor* (New York: Simon & Schuster, 2001).
22. J. Bowlby, *Attachment and Loss: Separation, Anxiety and Anger* (New York: Basic Books, 1973). See also M. Mikulincer, "Attachment Working Models and the Sense of Trust: An Exploration of Interaction Goals and Affect Regulation," *Journal of Personality and Social Psychology* 74, no. 5 (1998): 1209–1224.
23. C. Hazen and P. Shaver, "Romantic Love Conceptualized as an Attachment Process," *Journal of Personality and Social Psychology* 52 (1987): 511–524.

Chapter Five

1. Vincent R. Waldron, "Relational Experiences and Emotion at Work," in *Emotion in Organizations,* edited by Stephen Fineman (London: Sage Publications, 2000), p. 71.
2. In a study of incivility at work, Pearson, Andersson and Wegner found that persons who instigated incivility were three times as likely to have more power than those who were targets than they were to be peers or subordinates. Christine Pearson, Lynne Andersson, and J. W. Wegner, "When Workers Flout Convention: A Study of Workplace Incivility," *Human Relations* 54 (2001): 1387–1419.

3. Waldron, "Relational Experiences and Emotion at Work," p. 67.

4. Christine M. Pearson, Lynn A. Andersson, and Christine L. Porath, "Assessing and Attacking Workplace Incivility," *Organizational Dynamics* 29, no. 6 (2000): 123–137.

5. Bennet J. Tepper, "Consequences of Abusive Supervision," *Academy of Management Journal,* 43 (2000): 178–190. See p. 178.

6. This quote comes from a study that I did with Michele Williams of administrative staff, looking at how the quality of interactions with others at work shape attachment to their work organization.

7. Pearson, Andersson, and Porath, "Assessing and Attacking Workplace Incivility."

8. Debra Meyerson, "Feeling Stressed and Burned Out: A Feminist Reading and Revisioning of Stress-Based Emotions Within Medicine and Organizational Science," *Organization Science* 9, no. 1 (1998): 103–118.

9. Waldron, "Relational Experiences and Emotion at Work," p. 75.

10. Thanks to my colleague Kim Leary for this useful suggestion.

11. Steven J. Wolin and Sybil Wolin, *The Resilient Self* (New York: Villard, 1993).

12. Ella Bell and Stella Nkoma, "Armoring: Learning to Withstand Racial Oppression," *Journal of Comparative Family Studies* 29, no. 2 (1998): 285–296.

13. Michele Williams and Jane E. Dutton, "Corrosive Political Climates: The Heavy Toll of Negative Political Behavior in Organizations," in *The Pressing Problems of Modern Organizations: Transforming the Agenda for Research and Practice,* edited by Robert E. Quinn, Regina M. O'Neill, and Linda St. Clair (New York: American Management Association, 1999), pp. 3–30.

14. Peter J. Frost, *Toxic Emotions at Work* (Boston: Harvard Business School Press, 2003).

15. Wolin and Wolin, *The Resilient Self,* p. 149.

16. Wolin and Wolin, *The Resilient Self.*

17. Barry Holstun Lopez, *Of Wolves and Men* (New York: BT Bound, 1978).

18. For example, see Christopher G. Davis, Susan Nolen-Hoeksema, and J. Larson, "Making Sense of Loss and Benefiting from Experience:

Two Construals of Meaning," *Journal of Personality and Social Psychology* 75 (1998): 561–574.

19. In a study of people who suffered loss in apartment fires, survivors' ability to find positive meaning in the events was found to have had a significant impact on their coping success. S. Thompson, "Finding Positive Meaning in a Stressful Event and Coping," *Basic and Applied Psychology* 6, no. 4 (1985): 279–295; B. L. Fredrickson, "Cultivating Positive Emotions to Optimize Health and Well-Being," *Prevention & Treatment* 3 (2000); H. Tenne and G. Afflect, "Benefit Finding and Benefit-Reminding," in *Handbook of Positive Psychology,* edited by C. R. Snyder and Shane J. Lopez (New York: Oxford University Press, 2002), pp. 584–598.

20. Charles S. Carver and Michael F. Scheier, "Optimism," in *Handbook of Positive Psychology,* edited by Snyder and Lopez, pp. 231–243. See also Christopher Peterson and Tracy A. Steen, "Optimistic Explanatory Style," in *Handbook of Positive Psychology,* edited by Snyder and Lopez, pp. 244–256; and Martin L. Seligman, *Learned Optimism* (New York: Knopf, 1990).

21. C. R. Snyder, Kevin L. Rand, and David R. Sigmon, "Hope Theory," in *Handbook of Positive Psychology,* edited by Snyder and Lopez, pp. 257–276.

22. Jane L. Hodgetts and William H. Hodgetts, "Finding Sanctuary in Post-Modern Life," in *The Career Is Dead—Long Live the Career: A Relational Approach to Careers,* edited by Douglas T. Hall and Associates (San Francisco: Jossey-Bass, 1996), pp. 297–313. Quote is on p. 297.

23. Connie Gersick, Jean Bartunek, and Jane E. Dutton, "Learning from Academia: The Importance of Relationships in Professional Life," *Academy of Management Journal* 43 (2000): 1026–1044.

24. Victoria A. Parker, "Growth-Enhancing Relationships Outside Work (GROWS)," in *The Career Is Dead—Long Live the Career: A Relational Approach to Careers,* edited by Hall and Associates, pp. 180–195.

25. Hodgetts and Hodgetts, "Finding Sanctuary in Post-Modern Life," pp. 297–313.

26. Debra Meyerson and M. Scully, "Tempered Radicalism and the Politics of Ambivalence and Change," *Organization Science* 6, no. 5 (1995): 585–601.

27. Debra E. Meyerson, *Tempered Radicals: How People Use Difference to Inspire Change at Work* (Boston: Harvard Business School Press, 2001).
28. This example is built and fictitiously elaborated based on a 1992 Harvard Business Review Case Study by Lawrence Rothstein called "The Case of Temperamental Talent."
29. Deborah M. Kolb and Judith Williams, *The Shadow Negotiation* (New York: Simon & Schuster, 2000).
30. Kolb and Williams, *The Shadow Negotiation,* p. 42.
31. Roger Fischer, William Ury, and Bruce Patton, *Getting to Yes: Negotiating Agreement Without Giving In,* 2nd ed. (Boston: Houghton Mifflin, 1992).
32. Also recommended by Kolb and Williams.

Chapter Six

1. A special thanks to Laura Atlantis, who worked with me to identify features of organizations that signaled a context conducive to high-quality connections. Laura did an independent study on this topic and jump-started this whole chapter.
2. Charles A. O'Reilly and Jeffrey Pfeffer, *Hidden Value* (Cambridge, MA: Harvard University Press, 2000).
3. Roger Lewin and Birute Regine, *The Soul at Work* (New York: Simon & Schuster, 2000), p. 261.
4. Lewin and Regine, *The Soul at Work,* p. 120.
5. Susan Harter, "Authenticity," in *Handbook of Positive Psychology,* edited by C. R. Snyder and Shane J. Lopez (New York: Oxford University Press, 2002), pp. 382–394.
6. Lewin and Regine, *The Soul at Work,* p. 217.
7. Jody Hoffer Gittell, "Achieving Teamwork Within Groups: Relational Coordination in the Context of Routine Crisis," paper under submission, 2001, p. 17.
8. James Collins, *Good to Great* (New York: HarperBusiness, 2001).
9. Collins, *Good to Great,* p. 62.
10. Collins, *Good to Great,* p. 62.
11. Wayne Baker, *Achieving Success Through Social Capital* (San Francisco: Jossey-Bass, 2000).

12. Collins, *Good to Great,* p. 51.
13. Jody Hoffer Gittell, *The Southwest Airlines Way: Using the Power of Relationships to Achieve High Performance* (New York: McGraw-Hill, 2003).
14. Thanks to Chris Pearson for her push here to consider who is getting recognized and how often.
15. Collins, *Good to Great,* pp. 136–137.
16. For more on knowledge sharing, see Georg von Krogh, Kaz Ichijo, and Ikujiro Nonaka, *Enabling Knowledge Creation* (New York: Oxford University Press, 2000).
17. Carrie Leana and Denise M. Rousseau, *Relational Wealth: The Advantages of Stability in a Changing Economy* (Oxford: Oxford University Press, 2000), p. 11.
18. Mark Granovetter, "Economic Action and Social Structure: The Problem of Embeddedness," *American Journal of Sociology* 91 (1985): 382–394.
19. In Anthony S. Bryk and Barbara Schneider, *Trust in Schools: A Core Resource for Improvement* (New York: Russell Sage Foundation, 2002).
20. Roberto M. Fernandez, Emilio Castilla, and Paul Moore, "Social Capital at Work: Networks and Employment at a Phone Center," *American Journal of Sociology* 105, no. 5 (2000): 1288–1356.
21. O'Reilly and Pfeffer, *Hidden Value,* p. 133.
22. O'Reilly and Pfeffer, *Hidden Value,* p. 37.
23. Peter Salovey, John D. Mayer, and David Caruso, "The Positive Psychology of Emotional Intelligence," in *Handbook of Positive Psychology,* edited by Snyder and Lopez, pp. 159–171. See also Daniel Goleman, "Emotional Intelligence as Managerial Focus Has Been Popularized," in *Emotional Intelligence* (New York: Bantam, 1995).
24. For more detail about the importance of these competencies when seen as part of emotional intelligence, see Daniel Goleman, Richard Boyatzis, and Annie McKee, *Primal Leadership: Realizing the Power of Emotional Intelligence* (Boston: Harvard Business School Press, 2002).
25. Goleman, Boyatzis, and McKee, *Primal Leadership,* p. 251.
26. Von Krogh, Ichijo, and Nonaka, *Enabling Knowledge Creation.*

27. John E. Tropman, *Making Meetings Work* (Thousand Oaks, CA: Sage, 1996).
28. Von Krogh, Ichijo, and Nonaka, *Enabling Knowledge Creation.*
29. Jane E. Dutton, Ryan Quinn, and Robert Pasick, *The Heart of Reuters* (University of Michigan Business School Case, 2002).
30. Jane E. Dutton, Peter J. Frost, Monica Worline, Jacoba Lilius, and Jason Kanov, "Leading in Times of Trauma," *Harvard Business Review* (January 2002): 54–61.
31. Monica Worline, Jane Dutton, Peter Frost, Jacoba Lilius, Jason Kanov, and Sally Maitlis, "Fertile Soil: The Organizing Dynamics of Resilience," working paper, University of Michigan, 2002.
32. Thanks to Tami Gibson for pointing out this example to me. It was happening right around me and I was so stunned I hardly noticed the power of these norms of interpersonal helping.
33. Lewin and Regine, *The Soul at Work,* p. 121.
34. Baker, *Achieving Success Through Social Capital,* p. 178.
35. Lewin and Regine, *The Soul at Work,* p. 150.
36. See Michael G. Pratt and Anat Rafaeli, "Symbols as a Language of Organizational Relationships," in *Research in Organizational Behavior,* Vol. 24, edited by Barry M. Staw and Robert I. Sutton (Greenwich, CT: JAI Press, 2002), pp. 93–133.
37. Lewin and Regine, *The Soul at Work.*
38. Lewin and Regine, *The Soul at Work,* p. 157.
39. Salovey, Mayer, and Caruso, "The Positive Psychology of Emotional Intelligence."
40. Lewin and Regine, *The Soul at Work,* p. 314.
41. Peter J. Frost, *Toxic Emotions at Work* (Boston: Harvard Business School Press, 2003).
42. For more details on the Mountain Institute, visit their Web site at http://www.mountain.org/. In addition, a helpful description of the Mountain Forum, one of the collaborative ventures that the Mountain Institute enables, is contained in Kathryn M. Kaczmarski and David L. Cooperrider, "Constructionist Leadership in the Global Relational Age: The Case of the Mountain Forum," in *Organizational Dimensions of Global Change: No Limits to Cooperation,* edited by David L. Cooperrider and Jane E. Dutton (Thousand Oaks, CA: Sage, 1999).

43. Julia M. Wondolleck and Stephen L. Yaffee, *Making Collaboration Work: Lessons from Innovation in Natural Resource Management* (Washington, DC: Island Press, 2000).

44. David L. Cooperrider, "Positive Image, Positive Action: The Affirmative Basis of Organizing," in *Executive Appreciation and Leadership,* edited by Suresh Srivastva and David L. Cooperrider and Associates (San Francisco: Jossey-Bass, 1990), pp. 91–125.

45. This example is an extension of Dewitt Jones's description of being a photographer at *National Geographic Magazine,* and how its vision has affected his photographic practice. His viewpoint is depicted in a videotape called "Celebrate What is Right with the World" (St. Paul, MN: Star Thrower Distribution Corporation, 2001).

46. Cooperrider, "Positive Image, Positive Action."

47. James D. Ludema, "From Deficit Discourse to Vocabularies of Hope: The Power of Appreciation," in *Appreciative Inquiry: Rethinking Human Organization Toward a Positive Theory of Change,* edited by David L. Cooperrider, Peter F. Sorensen, Diana Whitney, and Therese Yaaeger (Champaign, IL: Stipes, 2000).

48. P. LaBarre, "Hospitals Are About Healing: This One Is Also About Changing Lives," *Fast Company* (May 2002): 64–78. Designer Weisman's question, p. 78; other quotes, p. 74.

49. My colleague Robert Quinn states the choice starkly, challenging us to confront what is required of ourselves to make real change happen. He poses the choice as one of deep change or slow death. See R. E. Quinn, *Deep Change: Discovering the Leader Within* (San Francisco: Jossey-Bass, 1996).

50. Karl E. Weick, "Small Wins: Redefining the Scale of Social Problems," *American Psychologist* 39 (1984): 40–49.

The Author

Jane E. Dutton is the William Russell Kelly Professor of Business Administration and professor of psychology at the University of Michigan. She joined the University of Michigan in 1989 after serving on the faculty of New York University for five years. She received her bachelor's degree from Colby College and her master's and doctoral degrees in organizational behavior from the Kellogg Graduate School of Management at Northwestern University. Dutton was former associate editor of the *Academy of Management Journal*, and coeditor of *Advances in Strategic Management*. Her research papers have won both the *Academy of Management Journal* Best Paper Award and the *Administrative Science Quarterly* Award for Scholarly Achievement. She is a Fellow of the Academy of Management. In 2001 she was named Distinguished Scholar for the Organization and Management Theory Division of the Academy of Management, and was also awarded the Senior Scholar Award by the University of Michigan Business School.

Dutton's research focuses on how high-quality relationships affect individuals and work organizations. She is interested in the transformative potential of relationships as they enable growth, identity, knowledge, change, and vitality for individuals. She also studies how organizational contexts enable relational capabilities of organizations that heal, build resilience, and foster human flourishing. She is a member of a research team that studies compassion at work (http://www.compassionlab.com). All her work connects to a new perspective on organizational research and management called *positive organizational scholarship.* Positive organizational scholarship seeks to understand how organizational contexts enable extraordinary behavior of individuals, groups, and organizations. She has just completed an edited book titled *Positive Organizational Scholarship* with Kim Cameron and Robert Quinn (Berrett-Koehler, 2003).

Dutton teaches an MBA elective titled "Managing Professional Relationships" as well as the core organizational behavior courses. She teaches a Ph.D. course titled "Relationships and Organizations." She also works in the Michigan program on Multidisciplinary Action Projects, which keeps her working with a variety of firms in different competitive contexts.

Index

benevolence components of, 81; mapping trust investments, 102–104, 103*e*; positive/negative examples of, 79–81; power of, 81–82; putting to work, 102–106; revealing your assumptions about, 102. *See also* Distrust

Trust assumptions, 100, 102

Trust building: challenges of, 98–102; described, 18; strategies for, 82–98

Trust building challenges: 1: bad history/past disappointments, 98–99; 2: terror of giving away control, 99–100; 3: misestimating others' sense that we trust them, 100; 4; personal trust and attachment styles, 101–102

Trust building strategies: avoiding check-up behaviors and surveillance, 96–97; avoiding punishing people for errors, 97–98; giving access to valuable resources, 92–93; giving away control, 89–92; using inclusive language, 87–88; not demeaning others, 89; self-disclosure, 85–87; sharing valuable information, 83–85; soliciting and acting on input, 93–95; trusting by what we do, 89; trusting by what we don't do, 95; trusting by what we don't say, 88–89; trusting by what we say, 83

Trust investments: assessing your own, 104, 105*e*, 106; mapping investments by others, 103*e*; recognizing others,' 102–104

Trust violations: damaging effect of, 98–99; example of, 79–80

Tyabji, H., 35–36, 86, 163

Tysdal, C., 58–59

U

University of Michigan, 94, 155

Uzzi, B., 96

V

Values: organizational, 140–141; regarding development of people, 141–142; regarding respect/dignity of others, 144–145; regarding teamwork, 141; regarding the whole person, 142–144

Vaughn, K., 130, 132, 133, 134

VeriFone, 35, 86, 142

VeriGift, 159

Virtual respectful engagement, 45

Vodosek, M., 92

von Krogh, G., 154

W

Wall Street Journal, 24

Wallace, S., 28–29

Weick, K., 172

Western Solutions, 7

Whetten, D., 42

Whole person, 142–144

Williams, J., 131, 132, 134

Williams, M., 38

Wolf pack analogy, 123

Wolin, S. (Steven), 123

Wolin, S. (Sybil), 123

Wondolleck, J., 165–166

Work capacity damage, 8–9

WPAG (working Parents Action Group), 129

X

Xerox, 12

Y

Yaffee, S., 165–166

Z

Zand, D., 94

Zander, B., 31

Zander, R. S., 31

Zena, 79, 80, 88